FOUR SEASONS
IN CROSS STITCH

FOUR SEASONS
IN CROSS STITCH

Jayne Netley Mayhew and
Nicki Wheeler

David & Charles

To Ian and Tim, thanks for all your love and support.
For Barry, Juliet and Leo

Page 1: *Sunflower Pincushion and Pot Lid (see chart on page 51).*
Page 2: *Sea Shell Hand Towel and Bath Mat (see pages 60–1 for instructions).*

A DAVID & CHARLES BOOK

First published in the UK in 1997

A catalogue record for this book is available from the British Library.

ISBN 0 7153 0486 0

Photography by Di Lewis
Book design by Malcolm Couch
Printed in Great Britain by Butler & Tanner Ltd.
for David & Charles
Brunel House   Newton Abbot   Devon

Contents

Introduction 7

Techniques and Materials 8

Introduction

Once again, the Devon countryside has proved to be an invaluable source of inspiration. In 'Four Seasons in Cross Stitch', our second book, Jayne and I have chosen the animals, plants and flowers that capture the essence of each season. The four sections, Spring, Summer, Autumn and Winter, each have a main picture worked in a mixture of silk threads and silk ribbon embroidery; these can be worked on their own, or together to form a set.

The projects for spring include mad march hares, spring lambs, chicks, piglets and rabbits, and delicate wild flowers. Summer designs show a beautiful riverside scene with ducks and dragonflies, brightly coloured tropical fishes and sea shells, and lush summer fruits and flower garlands. The autumn pages include a hedgehog, wild mushrooms, autumn leaves and an unusual design of an adder slithering amongst the autumn leaves. Winter is depicted by blue-tits feeding at a birdtable, an otter playing in the sea, and a mixture of winter flowers and foliage including Christmas roses, pansies, holly, mistletoe and ivy.

We have included designs which are suitable for stitchers of all abilities. For the beginner there are small farm animals, shells and fishes, toadstool trinkets, and winter flowers. Some designs, such as the adder and summer fruits, may look complicated, but are worked in whole cross stitches. Both have been worked in silk threads and tapestry wool, to show how adaptable the designs are. For the more experienced stitcher, the barn owl, which is the largest and most complicated design in the book, would prove to be an enjoyable challenge. Many of the designs are complemented by the addition of silk ribbon embroidery to work flowers, petals and leaves, whilst berries and sea foam have been worked in beads to give extra sparkle and texture.

Such a variety of designs and projects, suitable for the novice to the more experienced, provides no end of inspiration for gifts and ideas. We hope that you will have as much pleasure and enjoyment from this book as we have had working on it.

Some of the designs in this book are available as kit packs by Janlynn and can be obtained by mail order. Further details can be found on the stockists page at the back of the book.

Happy Stitching!

Jayne Netley Mayhew and Nicki Wheeler

Opposite: *A selection of autumnal ideas to stitch as the evenings draw in:* (clockwise from top) *the Adder Cushion (page 99), Autumn Leaves Pincushion (page 90), Fairy-ring Champignon Paperweight (page 94), Shaggy Ink Cap Address Book (page 94) and Chanterelle Trinket Box (page 94).*

Techniques and Materials

FIRST STEPS
Charts, Colour keys and Graphs

Each project in this book includes a colour photograph of worked designs, colour keys, charts, graphs and instructions for making up the designs as gifts and accessories. Some designs, such as 'Shells and Fishes' on page 59, are worked on fabrics with different thread counts, making the finished design either larger or smaller. 'Adder and Autumn Leaves', page 97, and 'Summer Fruits', page 52, are worked in both stranded cotton (floss) and tapestry wool (yarn), demonstrating just how adaptable designs and fabrics can be. You can experiment with designs by using beads and interesting threads or simply by changing the background colour, as we have done with the 'Autumn Leaves' cushion and pincushion on page 90.

All designs use DMC embroidery fabrics, stranded cotton (floss) or tapestry wool (yarn). The symbols shown on the colour key correspond to DMC shade codes. Each project lists the number of skeins required for each colour code together with a colour name, which is given for easy reference only – when purchasing threads, use the correct shade code numbers. Where appropriate, measurements are given in metric with the imperial equivalent in brackets. Always use either metric or imperial – do not try to mix the two.

HOW TO USE THE CHARTS

Each chart has been hand drawn in full colour, using colours that match the thread shades as closely as possible.

Each small coloured square on the chart represents one complete cross stitch. A half-square represents a three-quarter stitch. A coloured square with a circle drawn in the centre, marks the position for beads or French knots – the project instructions specify which to use. If you wish to use stranded cotton (floss) to work cross stitches or French knots rather than use beads, the code numbers for both are given.

In some cases, a French knot is represented by a small black spot, such as for the eyes of the baby animals on pages 35–39. Thin, broken black lines indicate backstitch. Small black arrows at the sides of a chart indicate the centre, and by lining these up you will find the centre point.

Some designs use silk ribbon embroidery, worked in straight stitch. This is indicated on the chart by a long oval, which is then repeated on the colour key, with the ribbon width, colour and code number.

Each colour area has a symbol and is outlined by a thin black line. The symbols correspond to those listed in the key at the side of each chart.

Some of the larger charts are spread over four pages with the colour key repeated on each double page.

To prevent mistakes, work systematically so that you read the chart accurately. Constantly check your progress against the chart and count the stitches as you go.

HOW TO USE COLOUR KEYS

Each colour key has a row of coloured boxes with a symbol inside each box. These correspond with the colours and symbols on the chart. The number at the side of each box corresponds to the DMC shade code. Some projects use silk ribbon and beads – the colour key lists the colour code numbers for both and the width of ribbon used. Ribbon widths are given in millimetres only.

HOW TO USE THE GRAPHS

Graphs are used to indicate where to place the designs on the fabric, for example, in the cot blanket on page 35.

Graphs are also used to produce templates (fig 1) for making gifts and accessories. Each square on the graph represents 5cm (2in). Transfer the template on to ready-printed dressmakers' paper, or draw your own graph paper. All templates have a 1.5cm (⅝in) seam allowance included.

At the back of the book you will find two pages of templates which provide pattern pieces for the baby animal toys from 'Down on the Farm', and the ears

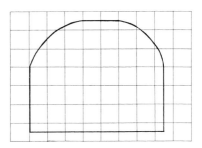

Fig 1: Template drawn on a graph

8

for the 'Fox Family'. The templates are drawn to actual size, and include a 6mm (^{1}/4in) seam allowance. These can either be traced or photocopied and cut out.

TECHNIQUES

Cross stitch embroidery is a simple and straightforward technique. The designs may look complicated but the effects are achieved by the clever use of colour and stitch work. Detail is added by using three-quarter stitch, backstitch and French knots and, in some cases, beads and metallic threads. Some designs also use silk ribbon embroidery to give added texture. Fine silk ribbon is worked in straight stitches for areas such as flower petals, leaves and feathers, giving a very delicate effect. The diagrams in the Stitch Guide, pages 11–13, show you how to work all stitches used. The following tips and techniques will help you gain a professional finish by learning how to prepare and care for your work.

PREPARATION

Each project gives the finished size of a design when worked on the recommended fabric, together with the amount of fabric needed. The fabric size is at least 8–10cm (3–4in) larger than the finished size of the design to allow for turnings or seam allowances when mounting the work or making it up into gifts. If making a garment such as a waistcoat, mark out the pattern pieces on to the fabric before you start stitching to ensure each design is correctly placed.

To prevent fabric from fraying, machine stitch around the edges or bind with tape.

Tack (baste) a row of stitches horizontally and vertically from the centre of each side of the fabric, to find the centre point from which to start stitching.

FRAMES

Mount the fabric on to an embroidery hoop or frame which will accommodate the whole design. Your work will be easier to handle and stitches will be kept flat and smooth.

Bind the outer ring of an embroidery hoop with white bias tape to prevent it from marking the fabric. This will also keep the fabric taut and stop it from slipping.

EQUIPMENT

Stitch your design using a tapestry needle, which has a large eye and blunted end to prevent damage to the fabric. Choose a size of needle which will slide easily through the holes of the fabric without distorting or enlarging them. You will also need a sharp pair of embroidery scissors, and will probably find it easier to sew if you use a thimble, especially for projects that use canvas.

STARTING OFF

To start off your first length of thread, make a knot at one end and then push the needle through to the back of the fabric, about 3cm (1^1/4in) from your starting point, leaving the knot on the right side. Stitch towards the knot, securing the thread at the back of the fabric as you go (fig 2). When the thread is secure, cut off the knot. To finish off or start new threads, weave the thread into the back of worked stitches (fig 3).

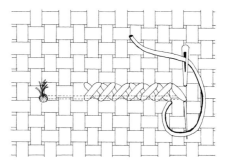

Fig 2: Starting off – knot on right side of fabric

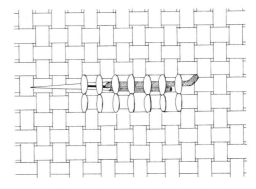

Fig 3: Weaving thread through back of stitches

WASHING AND PRESSING FINISHED WORK

If your work has become grubby during stitching, gently hand wash in warm water using a soft liquid detergent. Use a soft nail brush to remove any stubborn marks, rinse in clean water, place the damp fabric on a clean white towel and leave to dry on a flat surface.

Do not press directly on to your work as this will flatten the stitches and spoil the finished effect. Lay the work face down on a clean, white towel, cover with a clean, fine cloth and then press.

MOUNTING AND FRAMING
Take larger pictures to a professional framer, who will be able to stretch the fabric correctly and cut any surrounding mounts accurately.

For smaller pieces, back with lightweight iron-on interfacing to prevent the fabric wrinkling, and then mount into plastic flexi-hoops, trinket boxes or cards, following the manufacturer's instructions.

MAKING UP GARMENTS AND ACCESSORIES
When making up any item, a 1.5cm (⅝in) seam allowance has been used unless otherwise stated.

Instructions for making up are included under each project, where appropriate.

FABRICS AND THREADS

FABRICS
Most of the designs in this book have been worked on Aida fabric with 14 blocks or threads to one inch, this is often called 14-count Aida. Some designs use a larger or smaller count Aida or an evenweave fabric such as linen. The same design stitched on fabrics of different counts works up as different sizes. The larger the count (e.g. 18-count), the more threads per inch there are; therefore the design stitched on it will be smaller. The smaller the count (e.g. 6-count), the fewer threads per inch; therefore the design is larger.

One of the reasons why cross stitch is so popular, apart from its being easy to work, is that the designs are simple to adapt: merely by changing the fabric, the thickness or type of thread or the background colour a design can be transformed, and examples of this are given throughout the book.

Some of the designs are worked on very fine fabrics such as the pretty flower buttons, page 81, and foxglove door finger-plate, page 71. These can be very hard work on the eyes, so you could work the design using half cross stitch, or, alternatively, use an illuminated magnifying glass.

Each project lists the type of fabric used, giving the thread count, fabric name and DMC code number, which should be quoted when purchasing goods. All DMC threads and fabrics can be purchased from good needlework shops. The finished size of each design is also given, but you can experiment by using different fabric counts to achieve surprising effects. Before starting a piece of work, always check the thread and stitch count to ensure that the design will fit the frame for which it is intended.

THREADS
If you want your design to look exactly the same as those shown in the photographs, use the colours and threads listed for each project. The threads used in this book are DMC stranded cotton (floss), tapestry wool (yarn) and metallic threads. Silk ribbons, used for some of the designs, are available from Ribbon Designs (see Stockists, page 127).

Stranded cotton (floss) is a lustrous, 'mercerised' thread, which has a smooth finish and a slight sheen. It is made from six strands twisted together to form a thick thread, which can be used whole or split into thinner strands. The type of fabric used will determine how many strands of thread you will need to use; most of the designs in this book use two strands of thread for cross stitch and one strand for backstitch. Stranded cotton (floss) is the most widely used embroidery thread and is available in hundreds of colour shades.

Tapestry wool (yarn) is a matt, hairy yarn made from 100 per cent wool. DMC wool (yarn) is made from short fibres, twisted together to make a thick single thread which can not be split. Designs are usually worked on canvas using one or two strands. A wide selection of colours is available, although the shades tend to be slightly duller than for stranded cotton (floss).

Metallic threads vary quite considerably in texture and fibre content. Some are thick single threads made from a mixture of viscose, nylon and metallised polyester, whilst finer threads are often made from metallised polyester or Lurex and have a flat appearance.

Silk ribbon is made from 100 per cent silk, so very fine and soft that it is ideal for embroidery. It is available in widths as fine as 2mm up to 13mm, in a large variety of colours, and is sold by the metre or in different sized packs.

THREAD MANAGEMENT
Always keep threads tidy and manageable. Cut the threads to equal lengths and loop them into project cards, with the thread shade code and colour key symbol written at the side. A 'thread organizer' is pictured opposite.

STITCH GUIDE

When following instructions, please note that one block or thread refers to one block of Aida fabric or one thread of evenweave fabric.

CROSS STITCH

Each coloured square on the chart represents one complete cross stitch.

Cross stitch is worked in two easy stages. Start by working one diagonal stitch over one block or thread, then work a second diagonal stitch over the first stitch, but in the opposite direction to form a cross (fig 4).

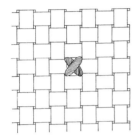

Fig 4: Cross stitch over one block of Aida or over one thread

A huge range of materials is available to the embroiderer, just a small selection is shown below.

The cot blanket on page 35 and the foxglove draught excluder on page 71 have been worked over two blocks or threads to give a larger stitch (fig 5).

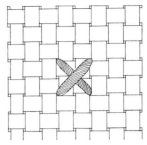

Fig 5: Cross stitch over two blocks of Aida or two threads

If you have a large area to cover, work a row of half cross stitches in one direction and then work back in the opposite direction with diagonal stitches to complete each cross. The upper stitches of all the crosses must lie in the same direction (fig 6).

Fig 6: A row of cross stitches

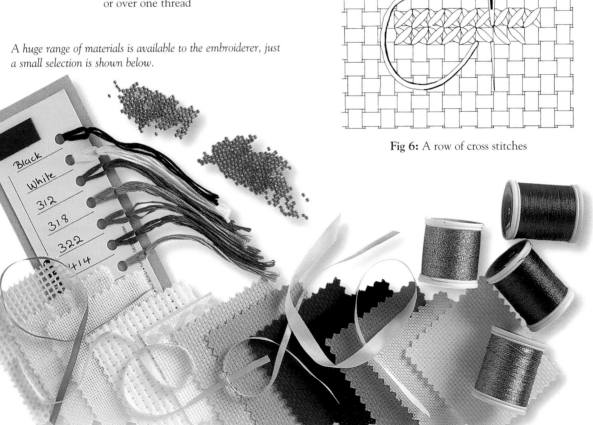

THREE-QUARTER CROSS STITCH

A right-angled triangle taking up half a square on the chart represents a three-quarter cross stitch. Work the first half of the stitch in the normal way, then work the second diagonal stitch from the opposite corner but insert the needle at the centre of the cross, forming three-quarters of the complete stitch. A square showing two coloured triangles indicates that two of these stitches will have to be made back to back (fig 7).

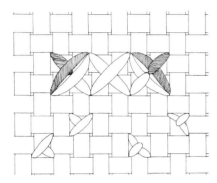

Fig 7: Three-quarter cross stitch

HALF CROSS STITCH

This stitch is used for the mice, brambles and berries buttons and brooch, page 81, because the fabric is so fine that a whole cross stitch would be too bulky. It is also used for the adder and autumn leaves firescreen on page 97, which is worked in tapestry wool (yarn). A half cross stitch is, simply, one half of a cross stitch, with the diagonal facing the same way as the upper stitches of each complete cross stitch (fig 8).

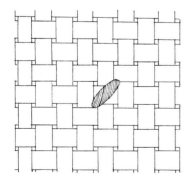

Fig 8: Half cross stitch

BACKSTITCH

Backstitch is indicated on the chart by a thin, broken black line. It is worked around areas of completed cross stitches to add definition, or on top of stitches to add detail.

To work this stitch, start by pulling the needle through the hole in the fabric at 1, then push back through at 2. For the next stitch, pull the needle through at 3, push to the back at 1, then repeat the process to make the next stitch (fig 9). This will give you short stitches at the front of your work and a longer stitch at the back.

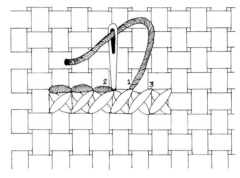

Fig 9: Backstitch

If working backstitch over two blocks or threads, such as on Afghan (Anne) evenweave fabric, work each stitch over two threads (as for cross stitch in fig 5).

FRENCH KNOTS

These are small knots which are used to add detail, for example, the animals' eyes on pages 35–39. They are indicated on the charts by a small black spot. Some designs, such as 'Mad March Hares' on page 18, use large areas of French knots – in this case they are indicated by a coloured square with a circle at the centre.

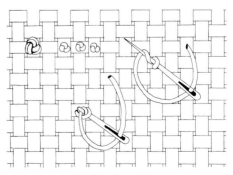

Fig 10: French knots

To work this stitch, bring the needle through to the front of the fabric and wind the thread tightly once around the needle. Hold the twisted thread firmly in place and carefully insert the needle one thread away from its starting position (fig 10). For a larger knot, twist the thread two or three times around the needle.

ADDING BEADS

Beads are indicated on the charts by a coloured square with a circle at the centre. With the needle at the right side of the fabric, thread the bead over the needle and on to the thread, then attach it to the fabric by working the first half of the cross stitch (fig 11). All stitches must run in the same direction so that the beads lie in neat rows on the fabric.

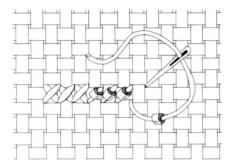

Fig 11: Adding beads

SILK RIBBON EMBROIDERY

Silk ribbon embroidery is indicated on the chart by a coloured oval. Work straight stitches over the amount of holes indicated by the length of the oval. Because the ribbon is so fine, it can be worked easily through the holes of the Aida fabric. Thread the needle as shown (fig 12) to secure the ribbon, ready for sewing.

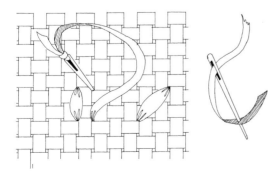

Fig 12: Silk ribbon embroidery

TECHNIQUE TIPS

✦ Steam press the fabric before stitching to remove any stubborn creases.

✦ Mount the fabric on to a frame to keep stitches flat and smooth.

✦ Work cross stitches with the top threads all facing in the same direction.

✦ Thread up lengths of several colours of stranded cotton (floss) into needles, and then arrange these at the side of your work by shade code number or by key reference.

✦ Work the designs from the centre outwards, or split them into workable sections such as quarters. On larger designs, first work the main subject and then complete the background.

✦ When taking a thread across the back of a design, weave it through the back of existing stitches to avoid any ugly lines showing on the right side.

✦ Use short lengths of thread – about 30cm (12in) – to reduce any knotting and tangling. Check your work constantly against the chart to avoid making mistakes

✦ For a smooth piece of work without any lumps or bumps, do not use knots at the back of your work, and cut off any excess threads as short as possible.

✦ If you are using several small designs to make up a larger picture ('Shells and Fishes', pages 59–63), plan the whole design before you start stitching. Photocopy the design charts, then cut out the shapes and arrange them on a large piece of paper. Use this as a placement guide when stitching the designs.

✦ Keep your work clean by packing it away in its own clean plastic bag to prevent any nasty accidents with spilt drinks, muddy paw prints or inquisitive fingers.

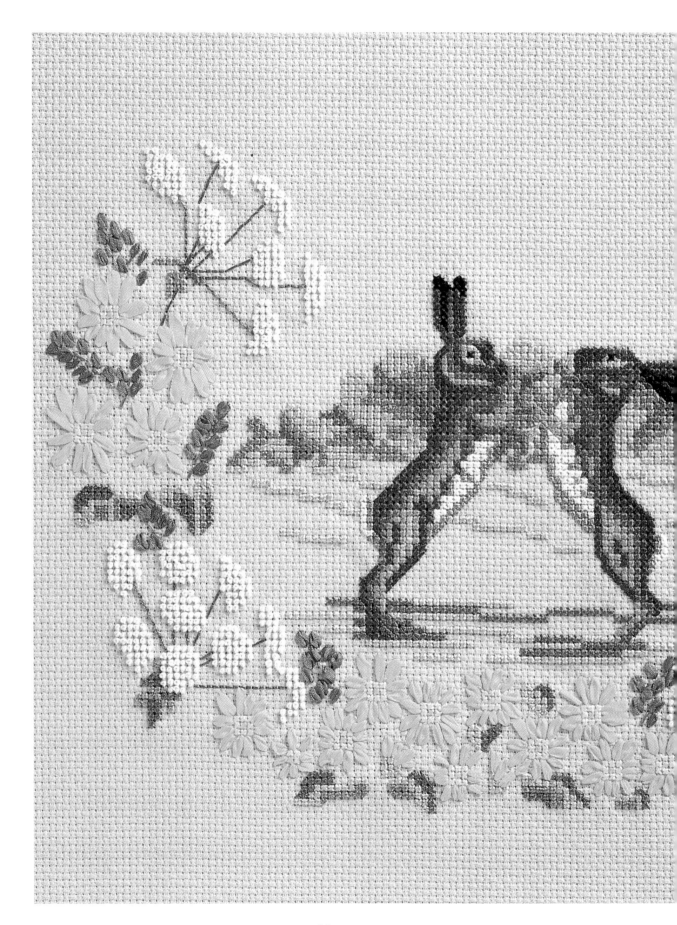

SPRING

Spring – when the sun starts to shine and the cold barren days of winter are soon forgotten. Flowers come into bud, leaves begin to sprout, and the fields and surrounding countryside seem to fill with baby animals. This explosion of new life inspired our main project, 'Mad March Hares' (opposite), worked in cross stitch with French knots and silk ribbon embroidery. 'Down on the Farm' (page 35), also inspired by this new life, is a delightful collection of baby animals decorating a baby's cot blanket, picture and cuddly toys.

In the 'Wild Flower Patchwork' collection (page 28), we used a delicate mixture of wild primroses, daffodils, violets and forget-me-knots to decorate a beautiful patchwork quilt and matching cushions.

Continuing the theme of spring flowers, dandelions – appropriately – appear on a stunning clock on page 24. The clock face, worked in Roman numerals, is surrounded by lush yellow and green foliage, whilst delicate fluffy seed heads float above. Finally, spring comes to a close with two delightful puffins nesting on a cliff top (page 40).

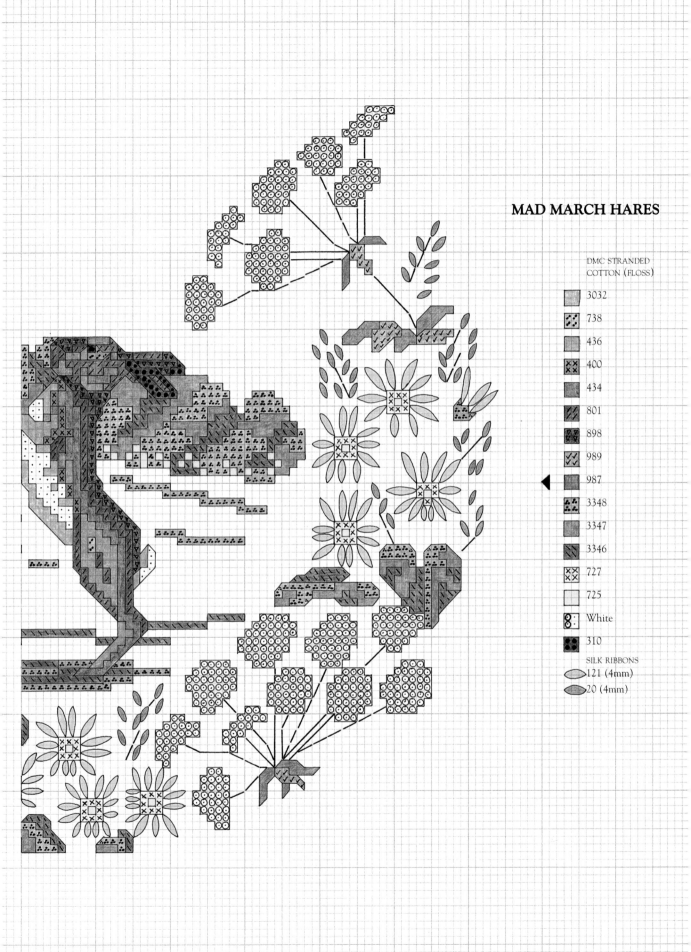

MAD MARCH HARES

DMC STRANDED
COTTON (FLOSS)

	3032
	738
	436
	400
	434
	801
	898
	989
	987
	3348
	3347
	3346
	727
	725
	White
	310

SILK RIBBONS
121 (4mm)
20 (4mm)

Mad March Hares

In a wonderful design to celebrate the coming of spring, the 'Mad March Hares' perform their courtship display framed by a beautiful floral border (page 16–17). The parchment-coloured Aida blends well with the tawny-brown and grey of the boxing hares, and in the pretty floral border silk ribbon embroidery adds extra interest and texture.

FINISHED DESIGN SIZE
19 x 26.5cm (7^{1}/$_{2}$ x 10^{1}/$_{2}$in) approximately

WHAT YOU WILL NEED
◆ Parchment 14-count Aida (Zweigart E3706), 38 x 46cm (15 x 18in)

DMC STRANDED COTTON (FLOSS)
1 SKEIN
Black 310; white; dark saffron yellow 725; light saffron yellow 727; med leaf green 3346; light leaf green 3347; very light leaf green 3348; dark forest green 987; light forest green 989; dark brown 898; med brown 801; very dark tan 434; med mahogany 400; med tan 436; dark cream 738; med brown-beige 3032

RIBBON DESIGNS SILK RIBBONS
4mm wide: yellow (colour 121), 4m (4^{3}/$_{8}$yd); olive green (colour 20), 2m (2^{1}/$_{4}$yd)

HARES

Hares have inspired many stories and superstitions: they have been seen as the creator of the Universe, as sacred to the Moon Goddess, and as a sign of fertility. It was also thought that witches could turn into hares to go out at the dead of night to secret meetings on secluded moors.

1 First, read through Techniques, page 9, and prepare your fabric. Refer to the Stitch Guide, pages 11–13, for how to work the stitches, and work the hares first, then the floral border. Finally, work the backstitch detail and then fill in the areas of silk ribbon embroidery.

2 Use two strands of stranded cotton (floss) for the cross stitch, backstitch and French knots.

3 Work the cow-parsley flower heads in white French knots. Work backstitch detail in dark forest green 987 for the cow-parsley stems, and light leaf green 3347 for the grass stems.

4 Work straight stitches in silk ribbon for the flower petals and the grass seeds of the border. The colours and widths of the ribbons are indicated on the colour key.

5 Refer to Mounting and Framing, page 10, for how to complete your picture.

Fox Family

*This amusing family of foxes will add fun to any breakfast table or tea-time treat.
The mother fox sits upright with her great brush tail wrapped in front of her, to make a wonderful
tea cosy shape. The naughty fox cubs licking their lips make cheeky little egg cosies.
Felt ears add the finishing touch to these delightful designs.*

FOX TEA COSY

FINISHED DESIGN SIZE
25.5 x 30.5cm (10 x 12¹/₈in) approximately

WHAT YOU WILL NEED
- Dark green 14-count Aida (Zweigart E3706), 48 x 52cm (19 x 20¹/₂in)
- Cotton fabric for backing, 43cm (17in) square
- Medium-weight polyester wadding (batting) 50 x 90cm (⁵/₈yd x 36in) wide
- Lining fabric 50 x 90cm (⁵/₈yd x 36in) wide
- Scraps of black and brown felt for ears
- Matching sewing thread

DMC STRANDED COTTON (FLOSS)
1 SKEIN
Black 310; medium mahogany 400; light cinnamon 402; charcoal 3799; charcoal grey 413; medium steel grey 414; chocolate brown 839; dark mink 840; light mink 842; dark flesh 945; medium flesh 951; very light pink-beige 543; peach 353

2 SKEINS
White; very dark brown 938; dark mahogany 300; light mahogany 301; medium cinnamon 3776; brown-black 3371

1 First, read through Techniques, page 9, and prepare your fabric. Refer to the Stitch Guide, pages 11–13, for how to work the stitches, and work the design from the centre outwards.
2 Use three strands of stranded cotton (floss) for the cross stitch and three-quarter cross stitch. Use one strand of brown-black 3371 cotton (floss) to work the whiskers in long straight stitches on top of the completed cross stitch.

TO MAKE UP THE TEA COSY
1 Use the graph to draw out a template of the tea cosy pattern (fig 13). Refer to How to Use the Graphs, page 8, for instructions. Place the template centrally over the stitched design, making sure that the bottom edge of the pattern is 2.5cm (1in) below the bottom embroidered edge of the fox. Cut one shape in Aida and one in cotton backing fabric. Also, cut two shapes each from wadding (batting) and lining fabric.

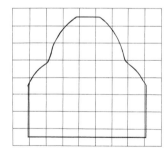

Fig 13: Tea cosy template

2 Lay wadding (batting) shapes side by side on a flat surface. With right sides up, place the embroidered Aida and the cotton backing fabric one on top of each wadding (batting) shape. Tack (baste) the fabric and wadding (batting) together to form the front and back of the tea cosy, working the stitches 1.5cm (⁵/₈in) from the outer edges. Tack (baste) as close to the embroidered edge of the fox's head and face as possible.
3 Trace the patterns for the ears from the full size templates on page 126. Cut two large ear shapes

from black felt, and two smaller ear shapes from brown felt. Place the small brown shape on top of the large black shape, so that the bottom edges meet. Make two pleats along the bottom edge (fig 14), then tack (baste) in place.

Fig 14: Fox ear

4   To attach ears, place ear shapes over the embroidered Aida with right sides facing, so that bottom edge of each ear shape matches the top edges of embroidered fox head. Pin and tack (baste) in place.
5   With right sides facing and wadding (batting) outwards, place the front and back pieces together. Pin, tack (baste) and machine stitch round the outer curved edges, as close to the stitched fox head as possible, using the tacking (basting) as a guide. Trim away excess wadding (batting) to 6mm (¹/₄in) from the seam line. Secure the wadding (batting) and

fabric at the lower edges by tacking (basting) close to the straight edges. Turn the tea cosy shape right side out, and the ears will stick up. Finally, turn up a 2.5cm (1in) hem along the bottom straight edge, and tack (baste) in place.
6   Pin, tack (baste) and machine stitch the lining pieces together along the curved seam, then turn up a 2.5cm (1in) hem and press. Place the lining inside the tea cosy shape, concealing all seam edges. Finally, pin both layers together along the straight hemmed edges, making sure to match the side seams. Finish the cosy by slipstitching the two hemmed edges together.

FOX CUBS EGG COSIES

FINISHED DESIGN SIZE
9 x 9cm (3¹/₂ x 3¹/₂ in) approximately

WHAT YOU WILL NEED TO MAKE FOUR EGG COSIES
 ◆ White 14-count Aida (Zweigart E3706), 46cm (18in) square
 ◆ Scraps of black felt for backing
 ◆ Scraps of brown and black felt for ears
 ◆ Scraps of lightweight polyester wadding (batting)
 ◆ Scraps of lining fabric
 ◆ Matching sewing thread

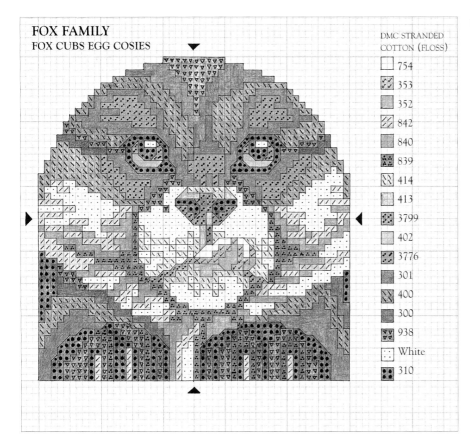

FOX FAMILY
FOX CUBS EGG COSIES

DMC STRANDED COTTON (FLOSS)	
□	754
⚹	353
▦	352
▨	842
▦	840
▩	839
▨	414
▦	413
⠿	3799
▦	402
▨	3776
▦	301
▩	400
▦	300
▽▽	938
⠂	White
●●	310

DMC STRANDED COTTON (FLOSS)
1 SKEIN
Black 310; white; very dark brown 938; dark mahogany 300; medium mahogany 400; light mahogany 301; medium cinnamon 3776; light cinnamon 402; charcoal 3799; charcoal grey 413; medium steel grey 414; chocolate brown 839; dark mink 840; light mink 842; light coral 352; peach 353; flesh 754

1 Follow step 1 for the fox tea cosy, working the design from the centre outwards.

2 Use two strands of stranded cotton (floss) for the cross stitch.

TO MAKE UP THE EGG COSIES

1 Cut around the embroidered shape, leaving 6mm (¹/₄in) around the curved edges and 1cm (¹/₂in) along the bottom edge. Use this as a template to cut one shape in felt backing fabric, and two shapes each from wadding (batting) and lining fabric for each egg cosy.

2 Follow the steps 2 to 6 of the instructions for making up the tea cosy, page 19. In this case, take a 6mm (¹/₄in) seam allowance all the way round and a 1cm (¹/₂in) hem along the bottom edges.

DMC STRANDED COTTON (FLOSS)

- 353
- 842
- 840
- 839
- 543
- 414
- 413
- 3779
- 951
- 945
- 402
- 3776
- 301
- 400
- 300
- 938
- 3371
- White
- 310

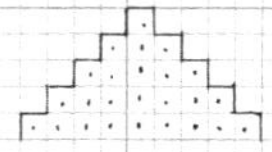

FOX FAMILY
TEA COSY

Dandelion Clock

Blowing the fluffy seeds from dandelion heads to tell the time is a delightful childhood memory, making dandelions the perfect image for our clock. The vibrant greens and yellows of the dandelion in full bloom give this design a beautiful richness, which graduates up to the delicate whites, creams and lemons of the dandelion seed heads. The design is worked in cross stitch with delicate backstitch detail used for the seed heads.

FINISHED DESIGN SIZE
13 x 18cm (5 x 7in) approximately

WHAT YOU WILL NEED
✦ Antique white 22-count Hardanger (Zweigart E1008), 33 x 38cm (13 x 15in)
✦ Mantle Clock (available from Framecraft, see Stockists, page 127)

DMC STRANDED COTTON (FLOSS)
1 SKEIN
Black 310; white; cream 3823; light saffron yellow 727; med saffron yellow 726; dark saffron yellow 725; light topaz 783; med topaz 782; very light leaf green 3348; light leaf green 3347; med leaf green 3346; dark leaf green 3345; light lime green 3819; very dark brown-beige 3031; med beige 642; beige 644; dark khaki green 3011; med khaki green 3012; hint of grey 762; light ash grey 415; light pink-brown 3064

1 First, read through Techniques, page 9, and prepare your fabric. Refer to the Stitch Guide, pages 11–13, for how to work the stitches, and work the clock face first, then work flowers and foliage around the edges.
2 Use two strands of stranded cotton (floss) for the cross stitch, and one strand of stranded cotton (floss) for the backstitch.
3 Work backstitch detail in med khaki green 3012 for the grass stems, and very dark brown-beige 3031 for the seed head stems. Work the Roman numerals for the clock dial in long straight stitches, using two strands of black 310.

4 When you have completed the design, refer to manufacturer's instructions for mounting the cross stitch into the clock case.

DANDELIONS
These bright yellow flowers have many names, including clock flower, blowball, and lion's tooth. Many stories and rhymes are associated with them, such as the old superstition that if you blow the seed head clean away, the number of blows will equal the number of years you will be married. One old fable says that dandelions were created by the dust blown up by the chariot of Phoebus the Sun God, and that, as the sun rises, the beautiful golden flowers open, and when it sets, the dandelions sleep.

This clock glows with the fresh colours of spring. The clock case and movement are commercially available, see the stockists list on page 127 for details.

DANDELION CLOCK

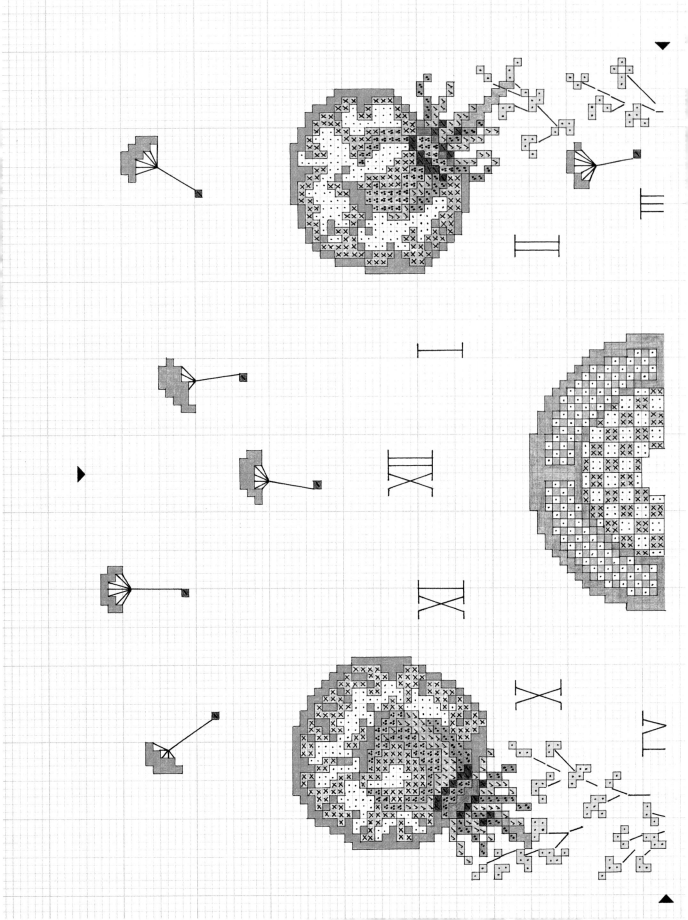

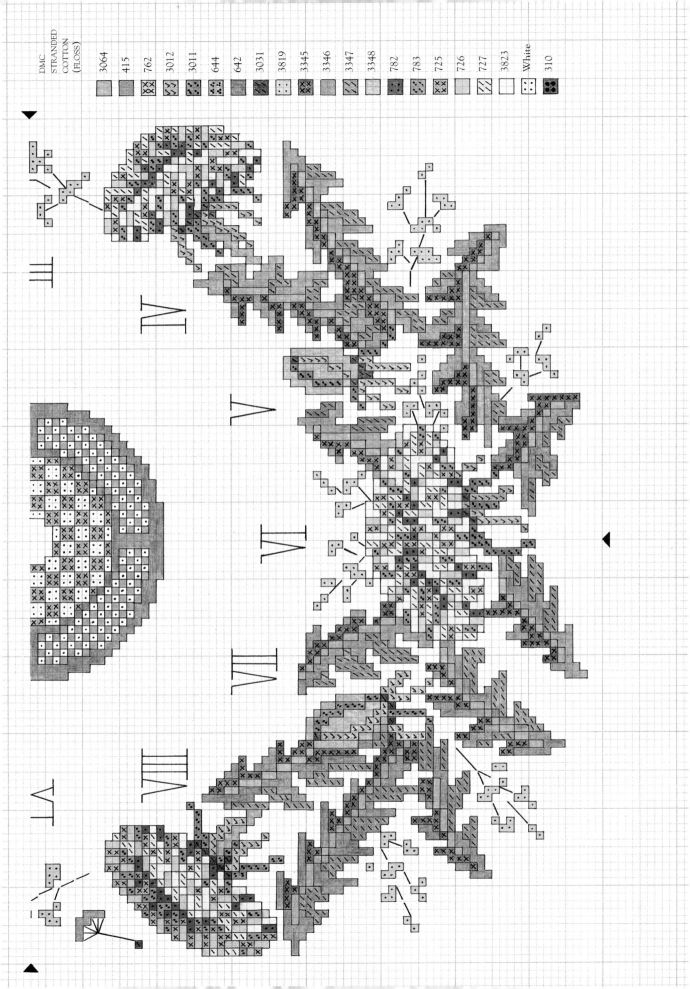

DMC
STRANDED
COTTON
(FLOSS)

3064
415
762
3012
3011
644
642
3031
3819
3345
3346
3347
3348
782
783
725
726
727
3823
White
310

Wild Flower Patchwork

We have taken beautiful primroses, daffodils, violets and forget-me-nots, and combined them with pretty fabrics to make a gorgeous patchwork quilt and matching cushions. The designs are each worked on a small Aida square, making them ideal for a variety of other needlework projects.

FLORAL PATCHWORK QUILT

FINISHED DESIGN SIZE
Each design measures 15cm (6in) square approximately

WHAT YOU WILL NEED
- ✦ Antique white 14-count Aida (Zweigart E3706), 1.4m x 110cm (1¹/₂yd x 40in) wide
- ✦ Fabric A (patchwork squares), 50 x115cm (⁵/syd x 45in) wide
- ✦ Fabric B (patchwork squares and outer border), 1.5m x 115cm (1⁵/syd x 45in) wide
- ✦ Fabric C (inner border, corner squares and edging), 1.5m x 115cm (1⁵/syd x 45in) wide
- ✦ Backing fabric 3.10m x 90cm (3³/syd x 36in) wide
- ✦ Lightweight polyester wadding (batting), 3.10m x 90cm (3³/syd x 36in) wide
- ✦ Matching sewing thread
- ✦ Quilting thread (optional)

DMC STRANDED COTTON (FLOSS)
1 SKEIN
Primrose – white; cream 3823; pale yellow 745; light yellow 744; med yellow 743; mustard 3820; med topaz 782; dark brown 898; med moss green 470; dark moss green 469; med avocado green 937; very deep avocado green 934; light terracotta 758;

Daffodil – dark saffron yellow 725; med saffron yellow 726; light saffron yellow 727; cream 3823; dark tangerine 740; med tangerine 741; light tangerine 742; dark mahogany 300; light mahogany 301; light leaf green 3347; med leaf green 3346; dark leaf green 3345; very dark leaf green 895;

Forget-me-not – white; med brown 801; med yellow 743; dark blue 825; forget-me-not blue 826; med blue 813; light dusty-rose 3716; med lavender 210; light leaf green 3347;

Violet – white; med saffron yellow 726; very dark cornflower blue 791; very dark lavender blue 333; dark lavender blue 3746; med lavender blue 340; dark jade green 3818; light jade green 3816

2 SKEINS
Forget-me-not – dark leaf green 3345;
Violet – med jade green 3815

The patchwork quilt is made up in stages, starting with the centre panel, then adding the borders. To make the quilt as shown, you will need a total of 17 embroidered floral squares – two primrose, three daffodil, six violet and six forget-me-not designs.

1 First, read through Techniques, page 9. Use a pencil to mark out 17 squares on the Aida fabric, each measuring 27cm (10³/₄in) square. Refer to the Stitch Guide, pages 11–13, for how to work the stitches, and then work each design from the centre outwards.

2 Use two strands of stranded cotton (floss) for the cross stitch. Use one strand for the French knots – very dark cornflower blue 791 at each violet flower centre, and med brown 801 at each forget-me-not flower centre.

3 For backstitch detail use three strands of stranded cotton (floss) in light terracotta 758 for the primrose stems, and light leaf green 3347 for the daffodil stems. Use two strands of med jade green 3815 for the violet stems, and white to highlight the forget-me-not petals.

4 When the squares are complete, cut away excess fabric so that each measures 21cm (8 1/4in) square, making sure that the floral design is central on each.

The soft blues and yellows of spring flowers compliment one another perfectly on these matching patchwork cushions and floral patchwork quilt.

WILD FLOWER PATCHWORK

VIOLET
DMC STRANDED COTTON (FLOSS)

- ◪ 3816
- ▨ 3815
- ▨ 3818
- ▨ 340
- ▨ 3746
- ▨ 333
- ▨ 791
- ▨ 726
- ⊡ White

PRIMROSE (below)
DMC STRANDED COTTON (FLOSS)

- ▨ 758
- ▨ 934
- ▨ 937
- ▨ 469
- ▨ 470
- ▨ 898
- ▨ 782
- ▨ 3820
- ▨ 743
- ▨ 744
- ▨ 745
- ▨ 3823
- ⊡ White

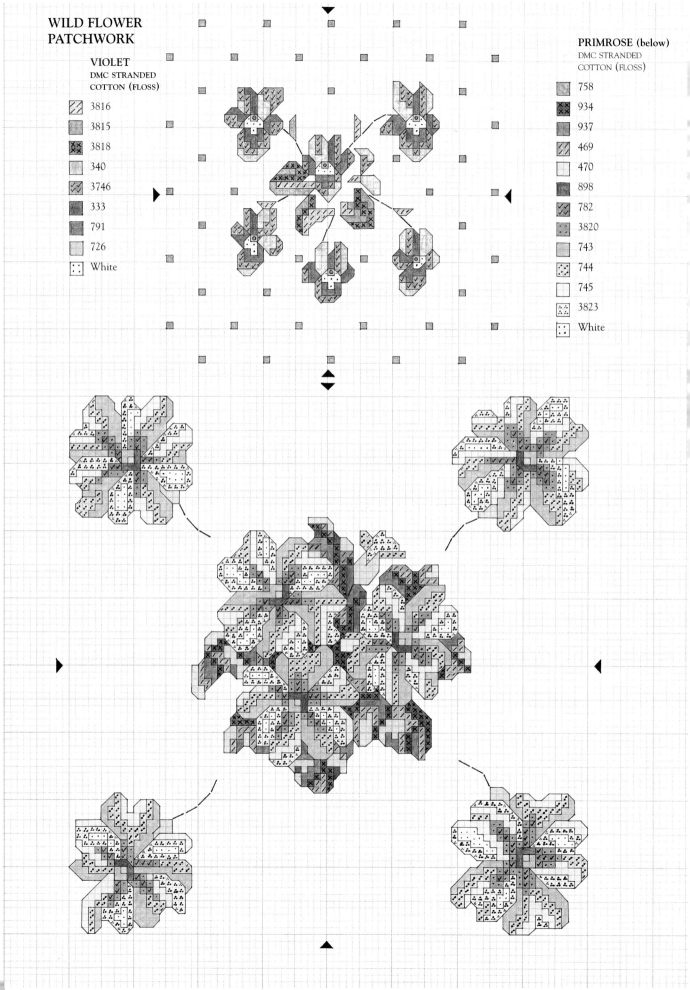

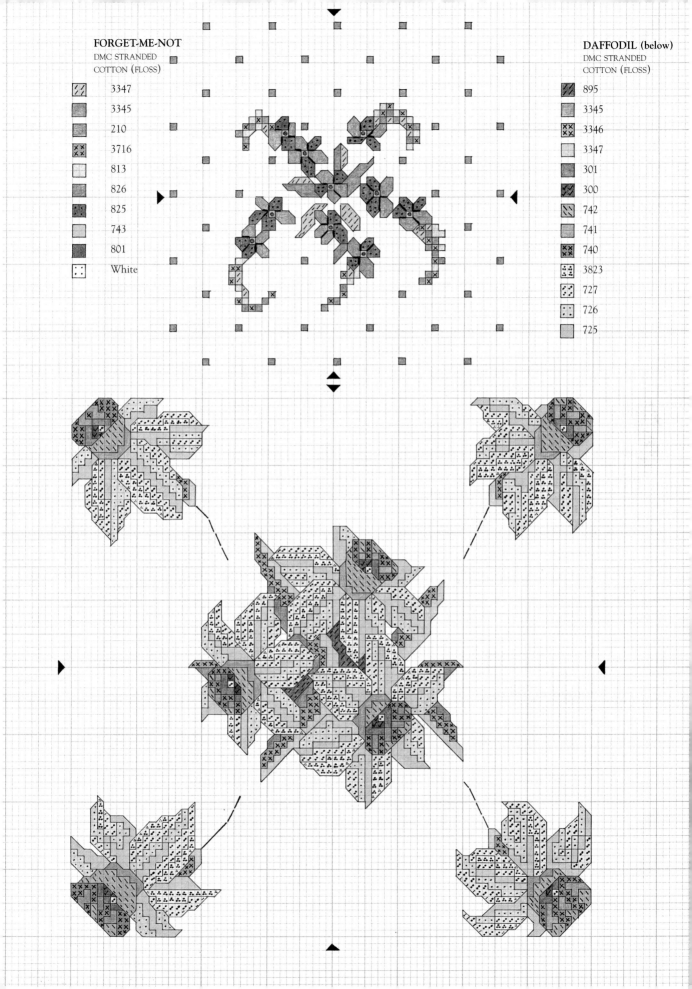

FORGET-ME-NOT
DMC STRANDED
COTTON (FLOSS)

3347
3345
210
3716
813
826
825
743
801
White

DAFFODIL (below)
DMC STRANDED
COTTON (FLOSS)

895
3345
3346
3347
301
300
742
741
740
3823
727
726
725

TO MAKE THE CENTRE PANEL

1 The centre panel is made up from 13 embroidered squares and 12 patchwork squares, with each patchwork square being made up from nine smaller squares of contrast cotton fabrics. The finished size of each completed square is 21cm (8 ¼in) square.

2 For the patchwork squares, make a template from thick card, measuring 9cm (3 ½in) square. Lay the fabric right side down on a flat surface, then use a pencil to draw around the template to mark out the shapes. Cut 60 squares from fabric A, and 48 squares from fabric B. It is important to be accurate when marking and cutting the fabric, so that the pieces will fit correctly when sewn together.

3 Arrange the nine fabric pieces for each patchwork square in the correct order by following the pattern layout (fig 15).

4 Each patchwork square is assembled from three strips of three squares each (fig 16). To make each strip, pin the squares together with right sides facing, matching the fabric edges, then pin and machine stitch 1.5cm (⅝in) from this edge (fig 16). Press seams open. When each strip is completed, join the fabric strips together in the same way, making sure that all the seam lines match (fig 16). Press seams open. Repeat this process until you have completed all 12 squares.

5 To complete the centre panel, refer to the pattern layout (fig 15) and arrange the 12 patchwork squares and the 13 embroidered squares in the correct order. The centre panel is assembled in the same way as the small patchwork squares, but has five strips of five squares each.

6 To make each strip, pin the patchwork and embroidered squares together with right sides facing, matching the fabric edges, then pin and machine stitch 1.5cm (⅝in) from this edge (fig 16). Press. When each strip is completed, join together in the same way, making sure that all the seam lines match (fig 16). When all five strips are joined together, press seams to complete the centre panel.

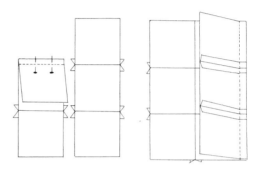

Fig 16: Making up squares from patchwork strips

TO MAKE THE BORDERS

1 For the inner border, cut four strips from fabric C, each measuring 21 x 93cm (8¼ x 36¼in) long, and use the four remaining embroidered squares.

2 Refer to the pattern layout (fig 15), to see how the border pieces should be arranged. The border is added following the same principle as the small patchwork squares and centre panel, by making up strips which are then joined together.

3 With right sides facing, pin and tack (baste) one long border edge to the top and bottom edges of the central panel (fig 17). Press seams. Take the two remaining border strips and, with right sides facing, pin, tack (baste) and stitch an embroidered square to each short edge, to form the corner squares (fig 17). Press seams. With right sides facing, pin, tack (baste) and stitch the three strips together to form one large patchwork square (fig 18). Press seams.

4 To make the outer border, cut four strips from fabric B, each measuring 129 x 15.5cm (50¼ x 6⅛in) long, and four squares from fabric C, each measuring 15.5cm (6⅛in) square. Join to the quilt in the same way as the inner border, following steps 2 and 3 above, but replacing the embroidered squares in step 3 with the squares cut from fabric C.

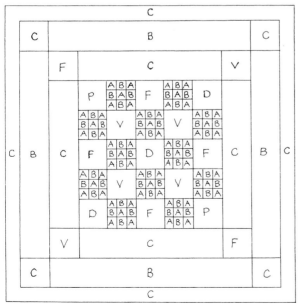

Fig 15: Layout for patchwork quilt
A–Fabric A; B–Fabric B; C–Fabric C; D–Daffodil;
F–Forget-me-not; P–Primrose; V–Violet

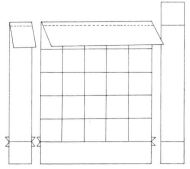

Fig 17: Attaching top and bottom borders to centre panel

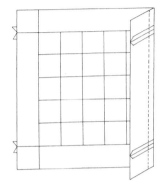

Fig 18: Attaching side borders to centre panel

BACKING AND FINISHING OFF

1 From the backing fabric, cut two lengths each measuring 154 x 78.5cm (61 x 30⅝in). With right sides facing, pin, tack (baste) and stitch the long edges together, so that the seam line runs down the of the centre of the backing fabric. Press seam open.

2 Cut two pieces of wadding (batting), each measuring 154cm (31in) long. Join the two lengths of wadding (batting) to form one large piece by butting the long edges together, and working a herringbone stitch (fig 19). Herringbone stitch the edges together on one side, then turn the wadding (batting) over and stitch the other side in the same way.

3 Lay the backing fabric, right side down, on a hard flat surface, lay the wadding (batting) on top of this, and then lay the patchwork front, right side facing

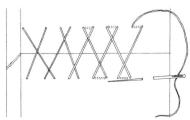

Fig 19: Herringbone stitch

upwards, over the wadding (batting). Pin the layers together, starting at the centre and working out towards the edges. Tack (baste) all three layers together in the same way, by starting at the centre and stitching lines which radiate from the centre outwards.

4 The patchwork can now be quilted, by hand or machine, using either sewing or quilting thread. The easiest way of doing this is to stitch along all the seam lines of the patchwork squares, to give each patchwork piece more definition, and to keep the wadding (batting) secure.

5 To finish the quilt, bind the raw outer edges. Use fabric C to cut enough 7cm (2¾in) wide strips to fit all the way round. Stitch the strips of fabric together to form one long strip. Press a 1.5cm (⅝in) hem along each long edge of the strip, then press the strip in half, so that the hemmed edges are enclosed inside.

6 With right sides facing, lay the binding on the right side of the quilt so that the first pressed hem is 2cm (¾in) from the outside edges of the quilt (fig 20). Pin, tack (baste) and stitch in place, mitering the corners as you go. Turn the border strip down and over to the back of the quilt to form an edging (fig 20). Hand stitch the edging in place at the back of the quilt.

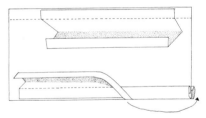

Fig 20: Attaching binding to quilt

PATCHWORK CUSHIONS

FINISHED DESIGN SIZES
Large design, 15cm (6in), small design, 7.5cm (3in) square approximately

WHAT YOU WILL NEED FOR EACH CUSHION
✦ Antique white 14-count Aida (Zweigart E3706), one 23cm (9in) square, and four 20.5cm (8in) squares
✦ Cotton fabric for backing, patches and frill 1m x 115cm (1⅛yd x 45in) wide
✦ Zip 30cm (12in) long
✦ Matching sewing thread
✦ Square cushion pad to fit

DMC STRANDED COTTON (FLOSS)
Use the list of threads for the Floral Quilt
forget-me-not and primrose

1 First, read through Techniques, page 9. Refer to the Stitch Guide, pages 11–13, for how to work the stitches, and work each design from the centre outwards.

2 For the centre motif, use six strands of stranded cotton (floss) for the cross stitch, backstitch and French knots, working over two blocks of Aida. Work the backstitch detail on the forget-me-not in white to highlight the flower petals, and work a French knot at the centre of each flower in med brown 801.

3 For each corner motif, use two strands of stranded cotton (floss) for the cross stitch and backstitch, working over one block of Aida. For the primrose, work the flower only, not the leaves and stem detail.

TO MAKE UP THE CUSHIONS

1 The cushion front is made up from five patches of embroidered fabric and four of contrast cotton fabric. Trim away excess fabric from the small corner patches so that each measures 13cm (5^1/$_4$in) square. Cut four pieces of cotton fabric, each measuring 13 x 23cm (5^1/$_4$ x 9in).

2 Make up three strips, each of three pieces (fig 16); refer to the photograph to arrange the pieces in the correct order. Pin the pieces together with right sides facing, matching the edges, then pin and machine stitch 1.5cm (^{5}/$_8$in) from this edge (fig 16). Press seams. When each strip is completed, join the strips together in the same way, making sure that all the seam lines match (fig 16). Press seams.

3 For the cushion back, cut two pieces of cotton fabric 23 x 43cm (9^1/$_4$ x 17^1/$_4$in). With right sides facing, pin and tack (baste) pieces together along one long edge, then stitch 5cm (2in) in from both ends leaving a gap at the centre. Neaten both long edges, then press seam open and insert zip following the instructions below.

4 For the frill, cut enough 12cm (4^3/$_4$in) wide strips along the length of the cotton fabric to give a finished length of 3.2m (3^1/$_2$yd). Make the frill by following the instructions below. With the patchwork fabric facing upwards, place the frill around the outer edge of the cushion front, so that raw edges face outwards. Distribute gathers evenly, then stitch in place.

5 Open zip slightly, then lay front and back squares together with right sides facing. Pin, tack (baste), and then carefully machine stitch along the stitching line, through all layers of fabric. Trim away excess fabric and neaten raw edges. Turn cushion cover to right side through the zipper opening and insert cushion pad.

TO INSERT THE ZIP

Stitch the cushion backs as described in step 3 of 'To make up the cushions'. Press seam open. Place the zip on to a flat surface, with right side facing upwards. Then, lay fabric, with right side facing, over the zip so that the pressed seam runs along the centre of the zip. Pin and tack (baste) along each side and both ends of the zip, then stitch into place using the zipper foot on your sewing machine. Remove all tacking (basting) stitches (fig 21).

Fig 21: Placing zip

TO MAKE THE FRILL

1 With right sides facing, stitch fabric strips along short edges to form a circle. Press seams open. Fold strip in half so that long edges meet, enclosing the raw edges of the short seams. Press (fig 22).

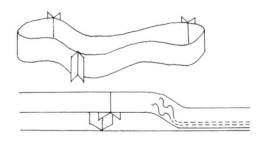

Fig 22: Making the frill

2 Run two rows of gathering threads along the raw edges of the fabric. Pull up gathering threads until the frill is the right length, then distribute gathers evenly.

Down on the Farm

*Spring is the time for new born animals, which is why we have used these delightful
designs of lambs, chicks, rabbits and piglets to decorate nursery accessories.
Each design is worked in a variety of cross stitch, three-quarter stitch, backstitch and French
knots, with a cross stitch border.*

BABY'S COT BLANKET

FINISHED DESIGN SIZE
12cm (5 3/4in) square approximately

WHAT YOU WILL NEED
◆ White 18-count Afghan (Anne) evenweave fabric
(Zweigart E7563), 74 x 114cm (29 x 45in)
◆ Matching sewing thread

DMC STRANDED COTTON (FLOSS)
1 SKEIN
Chicken – black 310; pale yellow 745; med yellow 743;
light tangerine 742; dark lemon 444; med pea green 906;
Christmas red 666; dark mahogany 300; dark orange-
spice 720 and med orange-spice 721; **Pig** – black 310;
very dark tan 434; coral 351; light coral 352; peach 353;
med pea green 906 and dark lemon 444; **Lamb** – black
310; white; grey-pink 453; med grey-pink 452; med pea
green 906 and dark lemon 444; **Rabbit** – black 310;
white; dark caramel 869; med caramel 420; light caramel
422; med pea green 906; dark lemon 444; peach 353
To stitch the cot blanket as shown in the photograph,
you will need: 3 skeins of med pea green 906; 2 skeins of
black 310, white, peach 353 and dark lemon 444; and 1
skein of each other colour.

1 First, read through Techniques, page 9, and
prepare your fabric. Refer to the Stitch Guide, pages
11–13, for how to work the stitches, and work each
design from the centre outwards.
2 Use three strands of stranded cotton (floss) for the
cross stitch, and work over two threads. Use two
strands for the French knots – black 310 for small
animals' eyes. Use two strands for the backstitch,
worked over two threads – black 310 around the
sheep and lambs, rabbits and chicken; dark

mahogany 300 around the chicks; very dark tan 434
around the pigs and piglets.
3 Afghan (Anne) is a soft evenweave fabric which
has tramlines running through it to create squares.
Cut a rectangle of fabric measuring 4 x 7 squares,
adding an extra 5cm (2in) all the way round the
outer edge to allow for fringing. Run several rows of
machine stitches 5cm (2in) from the outer edge.
4 Stitch the designs by following the pattern layout
(fig 23). Alternatively, stitch the designs at random,
or make up your own pattern. Work the borders for
the designs on the outside edge of the blanket in
med pea green 906; and for the designs at the centre
of the blanket use dark lemon 444.

Fig 23:
Layout for
cot blanket
S–Sheep
P–Pig
R–Rabbit
H–Hen

P			R
	S	H	
H			S
	R	P	
S			H
	P	R	
R			P

5 To finish, tease out the threads at the outer edges
to make a fringing. The rows of machine stitches
will prevent the fabric fraying further. Finally, make
tassels all the way round the edge by taking small
bunches of threads and tie them together in a knot.

PICTURE

FINISHED DESIGN SIZE
Each design is 9.5cm (3 ³/₄in) square approximately

WHAT YOU WILL NEED
✦ Cream 11-count Aida (Zweigart E1007)
30 x 60cm (12 x 24in)

DMC STRANDED COTTON (FLOSS)
Use the list for the cot blanket

1 Follow step 1 for the cot blanket. Instead of working a separate border around each design, work a continuous border all the way round the four animals, and one line between each design (see photograph opposite).

2 Use three strands of stranded cotton (floss) for the cross stitch. Use one strand for the backstitch and French knots.

3 Refer to Mounting and Framing, page10, for how to complete your picture.

STUFFED TOYS

FINISHED DESIGN SIZE
7.5cm square (3in square) approximately

WHAT YOU WILL NEED
✦ White 14-count Aida 23cm (9in) square for each toy
✦ Scraps of cotton fabrics or felt
✦ Polyester wadding (batting)
✦ Lightweight iron-on interfacing
✦ Matching sewing thread
✦ Black stranded cotton (floss) for eyes, nose and mouth

DMC STRANDED COTTON (FLOSS)
Use the list for the cot blanket

1 Follow step 1 for the cot blanket.

2 Use two strands of stranded cotton (floss) for the cross stitch. Use one strand for the backstitch and French knots.

3 Trim away excess fabric, leaving 2.5cm (1in) around each design. Cut the iron-on interfacing to the same size as the Aida square, and then carefully iron the interfacing on to the back of the design to give added strength to the fabric and help keep the stitches secure.

4 Trace the toy pattern pieces on pages 125–126; they include a 6mm (¹/₄in) seam allowance. For each piglet, lamb and rabbit, cut four arms, four legs, one back, one head and four ears from cotton fabric or felt. For the chick, cut one back and one head from the cotton fabric, and four wings, four feet and a small triangle for the beak, from yellow felt.

5 To stitch the eyes, nose and mouth, refer to the photograph, and the templates, and use two strands of black stranded cotton (floss). For the chick's beak, stitch the small felt triangle into place.

6 With right sides facing, pin, tack (baste) and stitch each pair of arms, legs and ears together along the curved edges, leaving the top straight edges open. Trim away excess fabric, then turn through to the right side. Lightly stuff the arms and legs. For the chick, pin and tack (baste) each pair of wings and feet pieces together, then stitch very close to the outer jagged edges, leaving the long straight edges open.

7 With right sides facing, match the upper edge of the embroidered fabric with the straight edge of the head piece. Pin, tack (baste) and stitch along the seam line, then press the seam open. Place the arms (wings), legs (feet) and ears over the body front, so that they face inwards and all raw edges meet. Pin and tack (baste) in place.

8 With right sides facing, match the back and front pieces together. Pin, tack (baste) and stitch along the sides and curved edges, leaving the bottom edge open. Turn to right side, through the gap at the bottom. Lightly stuff the head with wadding (batting), and then stitch along the seam line at the top edge of the embroidered fabric to keep the stuffing in place. Lightly stuff the rest of the body, and slipstitch the opening.

Each of the baby animal designs can be made into a cuddly toy, like the rabbit here or his friends pictured with the cot blanket, opposite.

DOWN ON THE FARM

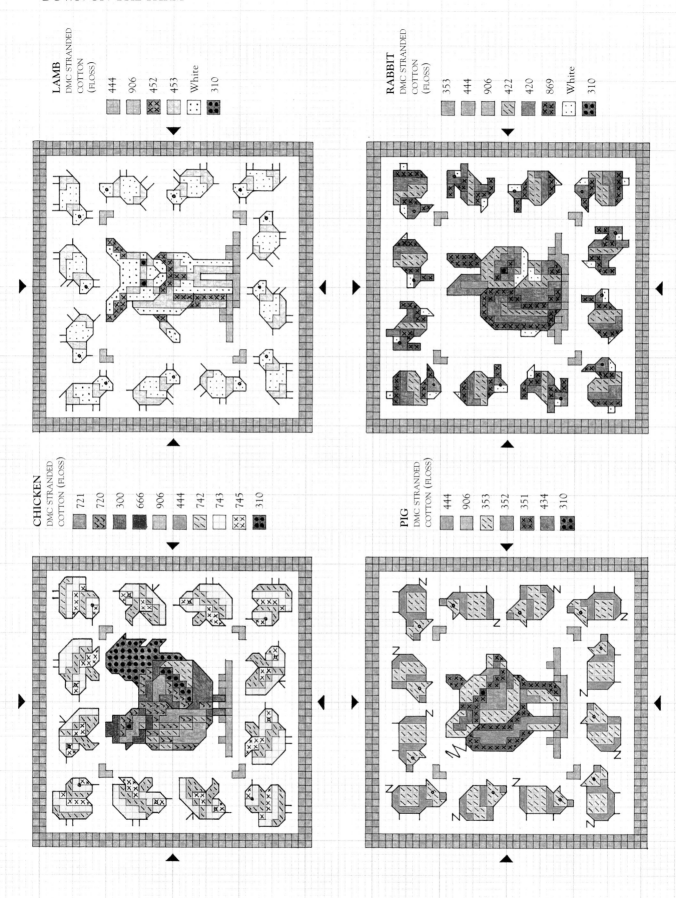

LAMB
DMC STRANDED COTTON (FLOSS)
444
906
452
453
White
310

CHICKEN
DMC STRANDED COTTON (FLOSS)
721
720
300
666
906
444
742
743
745
310

RABBIT
DMC STRANDED COTTON (FLOSS)
353
444
906
422
420
869
White
310

PIG
DMC STRANDED COTTON (FLOSS)
444
906
353
352
351
434
310

PUFFINS

Puffins

Puffins are exotically coloured for birds that live in such exposed northern coastal areas – bright red, blue and yellow beaks, and red feet contrast dramatically with the smart black and white body plumage. Our picture opposite shows a pair on a rocky ledge, surrounded by wild thrift. The pink flowers are worked in cross stitch, but could also be worked in French knots or embroidered with silk ribbons to give added texture and detail.

FINISHED DESIGN SIZE
19 x 23cm (7½ x 9in) approximately

WHAT YOU WILL NEED
♦ Grey 14-count Aida (Zweigart E3706),
38 x 43cm (15 x 17in)

DMC STRANDED COTTON (FLOSS)
1 SKEIN
Black 310; white; med rust 919; bright orange-red 606; bright orange 608; light tangerine 742; med yellow 743; light yellow 744; dark mahogany 300; med mahogany 400; very dark antique blue 3750; dark antique blue 930; med antique blue 931; charcoal 3799; charcoal grey 413; dark steel grey 317; med steel grey 414; light steel grey 318; light ash grey 415; beige 644; light beige 822; very deep pink 3687; deep pink 3688; pale pink 3689; light pine green 3364; med sage green 320; dark sage green 367; grey-pink 453; med grey-pink 452; dark grey-pink 451; med green-grey 3052; very dark brown-beige 3031; light mink 842; med mink 841

PUFFINS
The favourite habitats of the these comical little sea birds are coastal and off-shore waters. The puffin is small and stumpy, with a large leaf-shaped, yellowish bill which changes colour during the mating season to become a vivid striped red, blue and yellow – which could explain why puffins are sometimes called 'sea parrots'.

1 First, read through Techniques, page 9, and prepare your fabric. Refer to the Stitch Guide, pages 11–13, for how to work the stitches, then work the design from the centre outwards.
2 Use two strands of stranded cotton (floss) for the cross stitch and backstitch.
3 Work backstitch detail in light pine green 3364 for the flowering thrift stems, black 301 around each puffin's eye, eyeline and beak areas, and med steel grey 414 under the tail feathers. Work a French knot, using one strand of white, for the small highlights on the pupils of each eye.
4 Refer to Mounting and Framing, page 10, for how to complete your picture.

SUMMER

This collection of beautiful designs will help you to recapture the mood of those long idyllic summer days.

Our seasonal picture, 'Along the Riverbank' (opposite) evokes memories of lazy afternoons, idly chatting with friends over a picnic; while the simple 'Shells and Fishes' (page 59) bathroom accessory designs recall happy hours spent on the beach.

All summer long bright fragrant flowers bloom in our gardens, filling the air with their sweet fragrance and attracting fat bumble bees and dancing butterflies in search of nectar. Celebrate this floral abundance by choosing bright yellow sunflowers to create a delightful collection of accessories for the kitchen (page 47), or by working our flower garland of fuchsias, petunias and lobelia, into a cushion or tablecloth (page 64).

In 'Summer Fruits' (page 52), vibrant green bunches of grapes, lush red cherries, delicious apricots, oranges, pears and a mixture of juicy summer berries create a mouth-watering design that can be worked as a footstool or a rug. Whichever project you choose, these projects will bring a little of the season's warmth to your home any time of the year.

DMC STRANDED
COTTON (FLOSS)

	3753
	932
TT	646
XX	838
	436
NN	437
SS	676
	311
	415
	471
	3776
	918
//	703
	702
XX	699
	3078
RR	445
	307
	444
RR	720
	938
	3347
	3346
	3345
VV	744
	743
//	977
	976
VV	975
▲▲	898
	White
	310

SILK RIBBONS
20 (2mm)
127 (4mm)
36 (4mm)

Along the Riverbank

This tranquil scene conjures up memories of lazy summer days spent walking by the riverside. The richness of the dark chocolate-brown bulrushes and the bright yellow flag iris is complemented by the wispy grasses embroidered in silk ribbon. Floating down river in the background, the family of mallards is worked using one strand of thread, and this distant scene creates a delicate contrast to the rich foreground foliage.

FINISHED DESIGN SIZE
19 x 26.5cm (7¹/₂ x 10¹/₂ in) approximately

WHAT YOU WILL NEED
- White 14-count Aida (Zweigart E3706), 39 x 47cm (15¹/₂ x 18¹/₂ in)

DMC STRANDED COTTON (FLOSS)
1 SKEIN
Black 310; white; dark brown 898; chestnut brown 975; medium soft orange 976; soft orange 977; medium yellow 743; light yellow 744; dark leaf green 3345; medium leaf green 3346; light leaf green 3347; very dark brown 938; dark spice-orange 720; dark lemon 444; medium lemon 307; light lemon 445; very light golden-yellow 3078; dark Christmas green 699; dark brilliant green 702; medium brilliant green 703; dark rust 918; medium cinnamon 3776; light moss green 471; light ash grey 415; dark indigo 311; light old gold 676; light tan 437; medium tan 436; dark chocolate brown 838; medium smoke-grey 646; antique blue 932; very light antique blue 3753

RIBBON DESIGNS SILK RIBBONS
2mm wide: olive green (colour 20), 4m (4³/₈ yd)
4mm wide: rose pink (colour 127), 2m (2¹/₄ yd); brown (colour 36), 2m (2¹/₄ yd)

1 First, read through Techniques, page 9, and prepare your fabric. Refer to the Stitch Guide, pages 11–13, for how to work the stitches, and work the design from the centre outwards. Work the cross stitch first, add the backstitch detail and finally fill in the areas of silk ribbon embroidery.
2 Use two strands of stranded cotton (floss) for the cross stitch for the dragonfly, flowering rushes and foreground foliage. Use one strand for the cross stitch for the water, mallards, trees and riverbank forming the background area.
3 Use one strand of stranded cotton (floss) for backstitch. Use black 310 to outline the dragonfly wings and body, and the mallards and ducklings. Use dark brown 898 for the stems of the flowering rushes, and medium leaf green 3346 to work the stems of the grasses.
4 Use straight stitches of silk ribbon to work the flowering grasses and seed heads. The colours and widths of the ribbons are indicated on the colour key.
5 Refer to Mounting and Framing, page 10, for how to complete your picture.

ALONG THE RIVERBANK
In the summer, the river and riverbank team with wildlife, with an abundance of beautiful flowers and grasses. Colourful dragonflies dart though the air, catching insects on the wing, whilst the families of mallards and other waterbirds float gently downstream.

Sunny Sunflowers

Beautiful, bright sunflowers bring memories of warm sunshine and happy days, their bright yellow petals radiating like the rays of the sun. A mixture of cross stitch, three-quarter cross stitch, French knots and silk ribbon embroidery creates a lavish surface texture. For a more luxurious effect, work the designs on a rich blue Aida, as we have done with the pincushion and trinket pot lid pictured on page 1.

SUNFLOWER TEA COSY

FINISHED DESIGN SIZES
Design A – 5cm (2in) square, and
design C – 10cm (4in) square approximately

WHAT YOU WILL NEED
✦ White 15-count Aida band with yellow edging (Zweigart E7318), 1m x 6cm (1¹/₈ yd x 2¹/₂ in) wide
✦ Yellow 14-count Aida (Zweigart E3706), two pieces, each 23cm (9in) square
✦ Cotton fabric for tea cosy, 50 x 115cm (⁵/₈ yd x 45in) wide
✦ Lining fabric 50cm x 115cm (⁵/₈ yd x 45in) wide
✦ Medium weight polyester wadding (batting) 50 x 90cm (⁵/₈ yd x 39in) wide
✦ Matching sewing thread

DMC STRANDED COTTON (FLOSS)
1 SKEIN
Black 310; dark brown 898; brown 433; med golden green 581; dark golden green 580; dark avocado green 936; light tangerine 742; med soft-orange 976; chestnut brown 975; dark topaz 781; light topaz 783; dark saffron yellow 725; med saffron yellow 726; light saffron yellow 727; very light golden yellow 3078

RIBBON DESIGNS SILK RIBBONS
4mm wide: dark yellow (colour 15), 8m (8 ³/₄ yd)

1   First, read through Techniques, page 9, and prepare your fabric. Refer to the Stitch Guide, pages 11–13, for how to work the stitches, and work each design from the centre outwards. Stitch the cross stitch and French knots first, then the silk ribbon embroidery.

2   Fold the Aida band in half and cut into two lengths. Along each length, stitch a row of sunflowers using design A, repeated six times.

3   For the patches, embroider design C on to each square of yellow Aida, then trim away excess fabric to leave a 13cm (5in) square.

4   Use two strands of stranded cotton (floss) for the cross stitch and French knots.

5   Work the flower petals of design A in dark yellow silk ribbon.

TO MAKE UP THE TEA COSY

1   Use the graph to draw out a template of the tea cosy pattern (fig 24). Refer to How to Use the Graphs, page 8, for instructions. Cut two pieces each from check cotton fabric, lining fabric and wadding (batting).

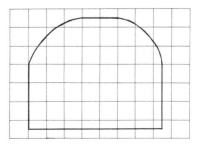

Fig 24: Tea cosy template

2 With right side up, lay the check cotton fabric shapes on a flat surface, then place each piece of Aida band right side up, on top of each shape, 5cm (2in) from the bottom straight edges. Pin, tack (baste) and stitch in place.

3 Pin and tack (baste) each patch diagonally above each Aida band, then run several rows of machine stitches 6mm (¹/₄in) from the outer edges. To finish each patch, make a frayed edging by teasing out the threads at the outer edges. The rows of machine stitches will prevent the fabric fraying further.

4 Lay wadding shapes side by side on a flat surface. With right sides up, place the check fabric shapes on top of each wadding (batting) shape. Tack (baste) fabric and wadding together to form the front and back pieces of the tea cosy.

5 With right sides facing and wadding (batting) outwards, place the front and back pieces together. Pin, tack (baste) and machine stitch round the curved edge. Trim away excess wadding to 6mm (¹/₄in) of seam line. Secure wadding and fabric at the lower edge by stitching 6mm (¹/₄in) from straight edges, then turn the cosy through to the right side. Finally, turn up a 2.5cm (1in) hem along the bottom straight edge, and handstitch in place.

6 With right sides facing, pin, tack (baste) and machine stitch the lining pieces together along the curved seam, then turn up a 2.5cm (1in) hem and press. Place the lining inside the tea cosy, concealing all seam edges.

7 Finally, pin both layers together along the straight hemmed edges, making sure to match the side seams. Finish by slipstitching the two hemmed edges together.

SUNFLOWER APRON

FINISHED DESIGN SIZES
Design B – 7.5cm (3in) square, and
design C – 10cm (4in) square

WHAT YOU WILL NEED
- ♦ White 14-count Aida (Zweigart E3706), 23cm (9in) square
- ♦ Yellow 14-count Aida (Zweigart E3706), two pieces, each 21.5cm (8in) square
- ♦ Plain yellow cotton fabric 70 x 90cm (³/₄yd x 36in) wide
- ♦ Contrast check cotton, 1m x 115cm (1¹/₈yd x 45in) wide
- ♦ Contrast bias binding, 1.10m (1¹/₄yd)
- ♦ Matching sewing thread

DMC STRANDED COTTON (FLOSS)
Use the list for the sunflower tea cosy, page 47

RIBBON DESIGNS SILK RIBBONS
7mm wide: dark yellow (colour 15), 2m (2¹/₄yd); light yellow (colour 12), 2m (2¹/₄yd)

1 Follow step 1 for the sunflower tea cosy, page 47. Stitch design C on the white Aida, and design B on each piece of yellow Aida.

2 Use two strands of stranded cotton (floss) for the cross stitch and French knots.

3 Work the flower petals of design B in silk ribbons. The colours and widths of ribbons used are indicated on the colour key.

TO MAKE UP THE SUNFLOWER APRON

1 Use the graph to draw out a template of the apron pattern (fig 25), marking the placement lines for the pocket and decorative patch. Refer to How to Use the Graphs, page 8, for instructions.

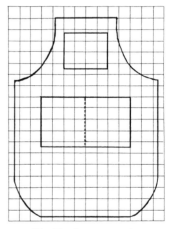

Fig 25: Apron template

2 Cut one apron shape from the plain cotton fabric. From the check fabric cut: one 28 x 43cm (11 x 17in) rectangle for the pocket; one 25cm (9³/₄in) square for the patch; one 10 x 66cm (4 x 26in) strip for the neck band, two 6 x 60cm (2¹/₄ x 23¹/₂in) strips for the waist ties; and four 10 x 100cm (4 x 40in) for the frill.

3 To make the decorative patch, press a 1.5cm (⁵/₈in) hem along all four edges of the check fabric square. Trim excess fabric from design C to leave a 13cm (5in) square.

4 Pin and tack (baste) the embroidered square diagonally on to the check fabric, then run several rows

Sunny sunflowers collection (clockwise from top): Apron, Cushion, Hand Towel and Tea Cosy

of machine stitches 6mm ($^1/_4$ in) from the outer edges. Make a frayed edging by teasing out the threads at the outer edges. The rows of machine stitches will prevent the fabric fraying further. To finish the patch, pin, tack (baste) and stitch in place.

5 For the pocket, press a 1.5cm ($^5/_8$ in) hem along all four edges of the check fabric rectangle, then machine stitch along one long edge to form the top of the pocket. Tack (baste) stitches through the centre of the rectangle, dividing it into two pockets.

6 Using design C on yellow Aida, follow step 3 to complete the pocket patches, then pin, tack (baste) and stitch the pocket in place, stitching along all but the top edge of the pocket piece, and along the row of tacking (basting) stitches across the centre.

7 For the frill, join the short edges of the strips to make one long strip. Press seams open, then turn up a 1cm ($^1/_2$in) hem. Stitch hem in place and press. Run two rows of gathering threads along the long raw edge. Pull the gathering threads until the frill is the right length, then distribute the gathers evenly.

8 With right sides facing, place the frill around the straight side and bottom curved edges of the apron, so that the raw edges meet. Pin, tack (baste) and stitch in place. Turn seam allowance towards the apron, press and keep in place with a row of top stitches.

9 Stitch bias binding around the remaining raw edges. Make the neck band and waist ties by folding the fabric strips in half lengthways, with right sides facing. For the neck band and ties, stitch along the long edge, and one short end of the ties. Turn to the right side and press. Stitch the neck band ends to the top corners, and the ties to the apron sides.

HAND TOWEL

FINISHED DESIGN SIZE
Design A – 5cm (2in) square approximately

WHAT YOU WILL NEED
◆ White 15-count Aida band with white edging (Zweigart E7316), 8.5cm (3$^1/_2$in) wide, to match width of towel
◆ Hand towel
◆ Matching sewing thread

DMC STRANDED COTTON (FLOSS)
1 SKEIN:
Black 310; brown 433; med golden green 581; dark golden green 580; dark avocado green 936; med soft-orange 976; chestnut brown 975

RIBBON DESIGNS SILK RIBBONS
4mm wide: dark yellow (colour 15), 5m (5 $^1/_2$yd)

1 Cut the Aida band to the width of the hand towel, adding 6mm ($^1/_4$in) turning at each end. Then, follow step 1 for the sunflower tea cosy.

2 Use two strands of stranded cotton (floss) for the cross stitch. Work the flower petals in design A in dark yellow silk ribbons.

3 Press from the wrong side, including the turnings at each end. Machine stitch the band to the towel.

SUNFLOWER CUSHION

FINISHED DESIGN SIZES
Design A – 5cm (2in) square, design B – 7.5cm (3in) square, and design C – 10cm (4in) square approximately

WHAT YOU WILL NEED
◆ White 14-count Aida (Zweigart E3706), four pieces, each 20.5cm (8in) square
◆ Yellow 14-count Aida (Zweigart E3706), 23cm (9in) square
◆ Check fabric for backing, patches and frill, 1.5m x 115cm (1$^5/_8$yd x 45in) wide
◆ Zip 30cm (12in) long
◆ Matching sewing thread
◆ Square cushion pad to fit

DMC STRANDED COTTON (FLOSS)
1 SKEIN:
Black 310; dark brown 898; brown 433; med golden green 581; dark golden green 580; dark avocado green 936; light tangerine 742; med soft-orange 976; chestnut brown 975

RIBBON DESIGNS SILK RIBBONS
4mm wide: dark yellow (colour 15), 1m (1$^1/_8$yd)
7mm wide: dark yellow (colour 15), 6m (6$^1/_2$yd); light yellow (colour 12), 6m (6$^1/_2$yd)

1 Follow the instructions in step 1 for the sunflower tea cosy, page 47.

2 To work the centre patch on yellow Aida, tack (baste) a row of stitches 5cm (2in) in from each edge of the square.

3 Work design A at the centre of the square, and design B at each corner, placing each design 1cm ($^1/_2$in) from the rows of tacking (basting) stitches.

4 For the corner patches work design B at the centre of each square of white Aida. When each design is complete, trim away excess fabric so that each corner square measures 13cm (5$^1/_4$in) square.

5 Use two strands of stranded cotton (floss) for the cross stitch and French knots.

6 Work the flower petals in designs A and B in silk ribbons. The colours and widths of ribbons used are indicated on the colour key.

TO MAKE UP THE CUSHION
1 To make the frilled cushion, cut four pieces of yellow checked fabric, each measuring 13 x 23cm (5$^1/_4$ x 9in), then follow making up steps 2, 3, 4 and 5 of the floral patchwork cushions, page 33.

2 To complete the cushion, insert a square cushion pad to fit.

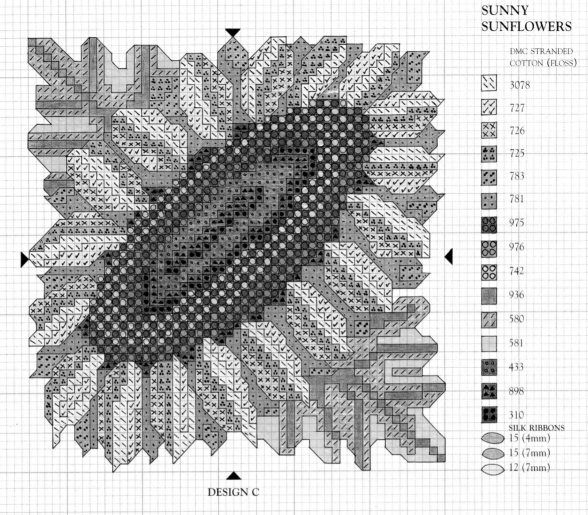

SUNNY
SUNFLOWERS

DMC STRANDED
COTTON (FLOSS)

⬊⬊	3078
✓✓	727
✗✗	726
♣♣	725
⦂⦂	783
⦁⦁	781
◉◉	975
◎◎	976
◐◐	742
	936
⫽⫽	580
	581
∷∷	433
▲▲	898
▦▦	310

SILK RIBBONS
⬭	15 (4mm)
⬭	15 (7mm)
⬭	12 (7mm)

DESIGN C

DESIGN B

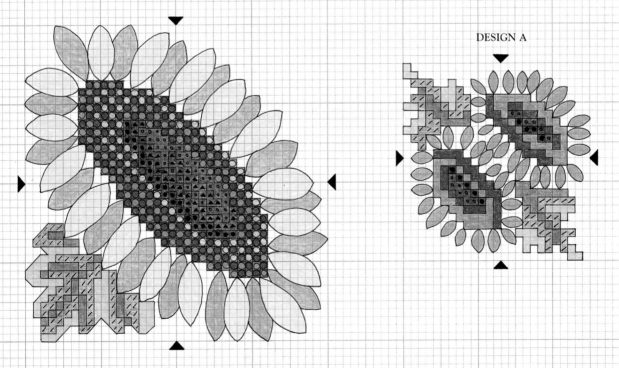

DESIGN A

Summer Fruits

*An abundance of delicious summer fruit
makes up this mouth watering design.
Set on a black background, the lush colours of
the ripe apples, pears, apricots, tangerines,
grapes and berries look irresistible. The design
is worked completely in cross stitch, making it
an ideal project to experiment with different
fabrics and threads. The beautiful footstool
worked in stranded cotton (floss) and the rug
worked in the richly coloured tapestry wool
(yarn) on canvas, show how versatile
cross stitch can be.*

SUMMER FRUIT FOOTSTOOL

FINISHED DESIGN SIZE
32cm (12¹/₂ in) in diameter approximately

WHAT YOU WILL NEED
◆ Black 14-count Aida (Zweigart E3706),
  56cm (22in) square
◆ 36cm (14in) diameter circular footstool

DMC STRANDED COTTON
1 SKEIN
Black 310; white; dark navy blue 823; dark violet 550;
very dark lavender blue 333; dark lavender blue 3746;
very dark avocado green 935; med avocado green
937; dark moss green 469; med moss green 470; dark
brass 832; very light moss green 472; light lime green
3819; dark golden green 580; dark green-grey 3051;
dark crimson 304; crimson 321; Christmas red 666;
very dark forest green 986; dark forest green 987;
med yellow-green 733; coral 351; med coral 350;
dark chocolate brown 838; very dark cornflower blue
791; very dark lavender 208; bright orange-red 606;
med ruby 601; dark sugar pink 603; med sugar-pink
604; light tangerine 742; med yellow 743; light
yellow 744; pale yellow 745; bright orange 900; very
dark orange 946; dark orange 947; dark tangerine
740; med tangerine 741

2 SKEINS
Med golden green 581

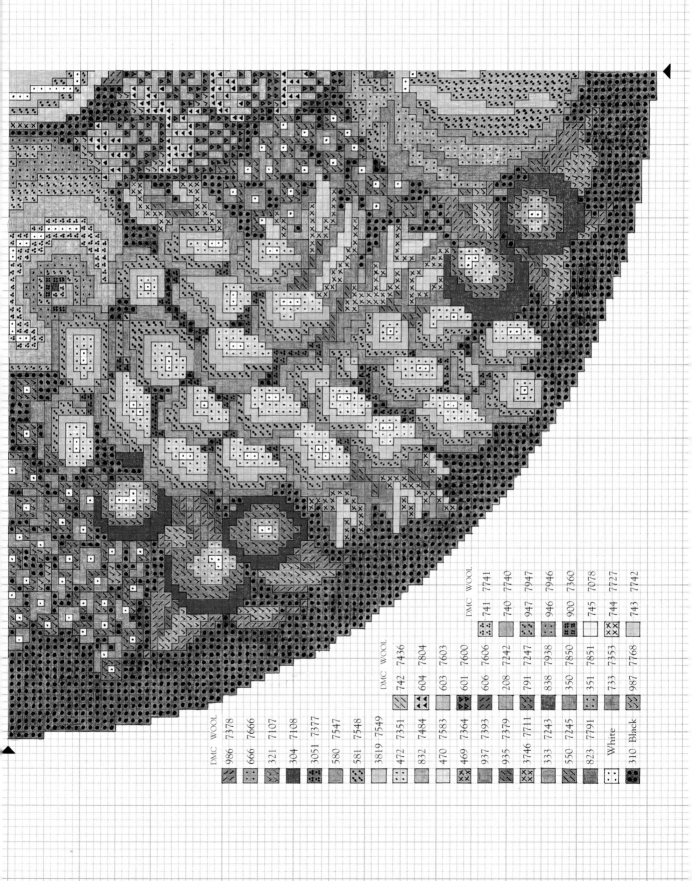

DMC	WOOL		DMC	WOOL		DMC	WOOL
986	7378		742	7436		741	7741
666	7666		604	7804		740	7740
321	7107		470	7583		947	7947
304	7108		601	7600		946	7946
3051	7377		606	7606		900	7360
580	7547		208	7242		745	7078
581	7548		791	7247		744	7727
3819	7549		838	7938		743	7742
472	7351		350	7850			
832	7484		351	7851			
469	7364		823	7791			
937	7393		733	7353		White	
935	7379		987	7768		310	Black
3746	7711						
333	7243						
550	7245						

SUMMER FRUITS

DMC	WOOL
741	7741
740	7740
947	7947
946	7946
900	7360
745	7078
744	7727
743	7742
742	7436
604	7804
603	7603
601	7600
606	7606
208	7242
791	7247
838	7938
350	7850
351	7851
733	7353
987	7768

DMC	WOOL
986	7378
666	7666
321	7107
304	7108
3051	7377
580	7547
581	7548
3819	7549
472	7351
832	7484
470	7583
469	7364

DMC	WOOL
937	7393
935	7379
3746	7711
333	7243
550	7245
823	7791
White	
310	Black

1 First, read through Techniques and following the advice given on page 9, prepare your fabric. Refer to the Stitch Guide, pages 11–13, for instructions on how to work the stitches, and then work the design from the centre outwards.

2 Use three strands of stranded cotton (floss) for the cross stitch.

3 When you have completed the design, refer to the manufacturer's instructions for mounting the cross stitch on to the footstool.

SUMMER FRUITS RUG

FINISHED DESIGN SIZE
79cm (31in) diameter approximately

WHAT YOU WILL NEED
- ◆ Ecru 6-count Sudan canvas (Zweigart E1124), 100cm (40in) square
- ◆ Large tapestry frame (optional)
- ◆ Tapestry needle
- ◆ Thimble

DMC TAPESTRY WOOL (YARN)
8M SKEINS
1 skein: med yellow-green 7353; dark chocolate brown 7938; light tangerine 7436; med yellow 7742; pale yellow 7078; bright orange 7360; very dark orange 7946; dark orange 7947; med tangerine 7741

2 skeins: dark lavender blue 7711; dark brass 7484; dark green-grey 7377; med coral 7850; bright orange-red 7606; dark tangerine 7740

3 skeins: very dark avocado green 7379; crimson 7107; Christmas red 7666; coral 7851; med sugar-pink 7804; light yellow 7727

4 skeins: white; dark navy blue 7791; very dark lavender blue 7243; dark crimson 7108; very dark forest green 7387; very dark cornflower blue 7247; very dark lavender 7242

5 skeins: dark violet 7245; very light moss green 7351; dark forest green 7768; dark sugar pink 7603

6 skeins: med ruby 7600

7 skeins: med avocado green 7393; med moss green 7583; dark golden green 7547

8 skeins: dark moss green 7364

9 skeins: light lime green 7549

11 skeins: med golden green 7548

38M HANKS
10 hanks: black

1 First, read through Techniques, page 9, and prepare your canvas in the same way. Rug canvas tends to stretch and loose its shape easily. To prevent this, and to make working easier, mount the work on to a large frame.

2 Refer to the Stitch Guide, pages 11–13, for how to work the stitches; work the design from the centre outwards. Use a large tapestry needle and use a thimble to protect your fingers.

3 Use two strands of wool (yarn) for the cross stitch.

4 When the design is completed, trim away excess canvas to within 10cm (4in) of the stitches. Fold the canvas turnings to the back of the rug, leaving 1.5cm (⁵⁄₈in) of canvas showing, all the way round the rug. Stitch the turnings in place.

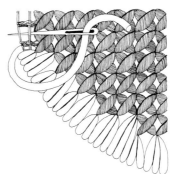

Fig 26: Overcast stitch

5 Finish the rug by adding an overcast edging. Using two strands of black, secure the thread at the back of the canvas, insert the needle in to the hole nearest the cross stitches, and pull to the front of the canvas. The overcast thread should share a hole with the last stitch of the cross stitch design. Take the needle to the back of the canvas and work the next stitch in the same way (fig 26).

SUMMER FRUITS
Not so long ago, supplies of summer fruit like these were limited and many were simply not available. Traditional farming techniques meant that fruits were only available for a short season, with huge gluts ripening at the same time. The fruits then had to be made into jams and jellies, or preserved in jars to be used later in the year. Today, we are quite spoilt for choice, with all sorts of strange and exotic fruits available from all over the world, all year round.

Shells and Fishes

Exquisite tropical fish drift serenely through coral and sea grasses, over starfish and shells, through crystal clear seas which sparkle in the white hot sun. The seashore picture on 14-count Aida is transformed when worked on larger 6-count Zweibinca for the bath mat. Smaller versions of the large bath mat shells look perfect decorating the hand towel. Using Aida Plus, your fish can become a mobile, swimming gently overhead.

Rather than give you a chart for each project, we've given you the charts for each element – fish, sea-horses, coral, shells – so that you can plan your own designs. Design tip: photocopy the charts, then cut them up and arrange them on a large piece of paper until you're happy with the arrangement. Our photographs should give you some inspiration!

DMC STRANDED COTTON (FLOSS) FOR EACH ELEMENT
1 SKEIN

Seahorse – black 310; white; dark fawn 611; dark yellow-beige 3045; med yellow-beige 3046; light yellow-beige 3047. Work backstitch detail using black 310 around the sea horse eye and body.
Starfish – light coral 352; coral 351; med coral 350. Work backstitch detail using med coral 350 around each starfish shape
Coral – light blue 827; light beige 822; beige 644; med beige 642
Sea grass – light forest green 989; med forest green 988; dark forest green 987; very dark forest green 986
Tower shell – med brown 801; very dark tan 434; med soft orange 976; dark pink-brown 3772; dark flesh 945; med flesh 951. Work backstitch detail using med brown 801 around shell and its spirals
Whelk – white; very light old gold 677; light old gold 676; med old gold 729; dark chocolate brown 838; med grey-brown 3023; med fawn 612; dark fawn 611 Work backstitch detail using dark fawn 611 around shell and its spirals
Top shell – white; very dark pink-brown 632; light pink-brown 3064; med flesh 951; very light flesh 3770; light steel grey 318; light ash grey 415. Work backstitch detail using very dark pink-brown 632 around shell and its spirals

Scallop – very light terracotta 3779; light terracotta 758; med terracotta 3778; dark terracotta 356; brick red 355. Work backstitch detail using brick red 355 around shell and its scallops
Powder-blue surgeon – black 310; white; light baby blue 775; dark lemon 444; med brown 801; light peacock blue 3766; med peacock blue 807; dark peacock blue 806. Work backstitch detail using black 310 around body and fin, and light baby blue 775 around each eye
Wimple fish – black 310; white; light baby blue 775; dark lemon 444; med lemon 307; med brown 801; beige 644. Work backstitch detail using black 310 around body and fin, and light baby blue 775 around each eye
Long-snouted coral fish – black 310; white; light baby blue 775; dark lemon 444; med lemon 307; light lemon 445; light topaz 783. Work backstitch detail using black 310 around body and fin, and light baby blue 775 around each eye.
Humbug fish – black 310; white; light baby blue 775; light steel grey 318; med brown 801. Work backstitch detail using black 310 around body and fin, and light baby blue 775 around each eye.

SEASHORE PICTURE

FINISHED DESIGN SIZE
Each design is 3.5cm (1^1/$_2$ in) square approximately

WHAT YOU WILL NEED
♦ White 14-count Aida (Zweigart E3706), the size of your finished design, adding 9cm (3^1/$_2$ in) for turnings all the way round

1 First, read through Techniques, page 9, and prepare your fabric. Refer to the Stitch Guide, pages

11–13, for how to work the stitches, and work the design from the centre outwards.

2 Use two strands of stranded cotton (floss) for the cross stitch, and one for the backstitch.

3 Refer to Mounting and Framing, page 10, for how to complete your picture.

SEASHORE BATH MAT

FINISHED DESIGN SIZE
Each design is 7.5cm (3in) square approximately

WHAT YOU WILL NEED
- ✦ White 6-count Zweibinca (Zweigart E3712), the size of your finished design, adding a 9cm (3¹/₂ in) seam allowance all the way round
- ✦ Cotton fabric for backing
- ✦ Medium weight iron-on interfacing
- ✦ Lightweight polyester wadding (batting)
- ✦ Matching sewing thread

1 Follow step 1 for the seashore picture above.

2 Use six strands of stranded cotton (floss) for the cross stitch, and two strands for the backstitch.

3 To make up the bath mat, carefully trim away any excess fabric to within 3.5cm (1¹/₂ in) of the completed design. Cut a piece of iron-on interfacing to the same size, then carefully iron the interfacing on to the back of the design to give added strength to the fabric and help keep the embroidered stitches secure.

4 Cut the backing fabric and polyester wadding (batting) to the same size as the embroidered fabric. Place the cotton backing fabric right side down on a flat surface. Lay the wadding (batting) on top, then pin and tack (baste) the two layers together.

5 With right sides facing and wadding (batting) outwards, pin and tack (baste) the front and back bath mat pieces together. Taking a 1.5cm (⁵/₈ in) seam allowance, machine stitch all the layers together, leaving a gap along one short edge for turning. Trim away excess wadding to 6mm (¹/₄ in), and trim fabric diagonally across each corner. Turn bath mat through to right side, then secure the opening with slipstitch.

6 Finish by adding several rows of topstitching close to the edges to strengthen them.

FISH MOBILE

FINISHED DESIGN SIZE
Large fish, 8cm (3¹/₄in) square, small fish,
3.5cm (1 ¹/₂in) square approximately

WHAT YOU WILL NEED
- ✦ White Aida Plus, three sheets
- ✦ Wooden or plastic hoop 15cm (6in) diameter
- ✦ Clear nylon thread
- ✦ Matching sewing thread

DMC STRANDED COTTON (FLOSS)
Use the list of threads for each fish, using two skeins of
light baby blue 775 and dark lemon 444, three skeins of
white, four skeins of black and one skein of each other
colour

1 Each fish is made from two embroidered shapes,
one the mirror image of the other, sewn back to
back. To reverse the charts for the mirror images,
photocopy them in reverse. Then, follow step 1 for
the seashore picture above.
2 Aida Plus is a specially treated Aida fabric which
allows you to cut out shapes without the fabric fraying. Because the cloth is stiff, you do not need to use
an embroidery hoop.
3 For the small fishes, use two strands of stranded
cotton (floss) for the cross stitch, and one strand for
the backstitch. For the larger fishes, use six strands
for the cross stitch, and two strands for the
backstitch, working over two blocks of Aida.
4 Place each matching pair of fish together, with
wrong sides together. Hand stitch around the outer
edge of the designs using matching thread. Cut away
excess fabric close to the stitching line, taking care
not to cut any of the stitches.
5 Paint the hoop, or cover it in ribbon, to match
the colours of the design. Attach a length of nylon
thread to each fish, then tie each thread to the hoop,
varying the lengths of each thread so that the fishes
hang at different heights. Attach three equal lengths
of thread to the top of the hoop, then tie these
together at the centre. Finally, tie a hanging loop to
hang the mobile.

Opposite: Seashore Picture
Above right: Fish Mobile
*Note: The Sea Shell Hand Towel and Bath Mat are pictured
on page 2.*

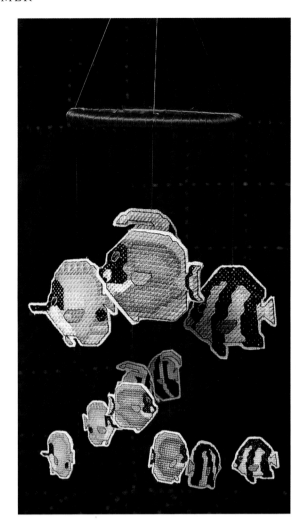

SEA SHELL HAND TOWEL

FINISHED DESIGN SIZE
3cm (1¹/₄in) square approximately

WHAT YOU WILL NEED
- ✦ White 15-count Aida band with white edging
  (Zweigart E7316), 8.5cm (3¹/₂in) wide, to match
  width of towel
- ✦ Hand towel
- ✦ Matching thread

1 Cut the Aida band to the width of the hand
towel, adding 6mm (¹/₄in) turning at each end.
Then, follow step 1 for the seashore picture.
2 Use two strands of stranded cotton (floss) for the
cross stitch, and one strand for the backstitch.
3 Press the band from the wrong side, pressing the
turnings at each end. Machine stitch the band to the
hand towel.

SHELLS AND FISHES

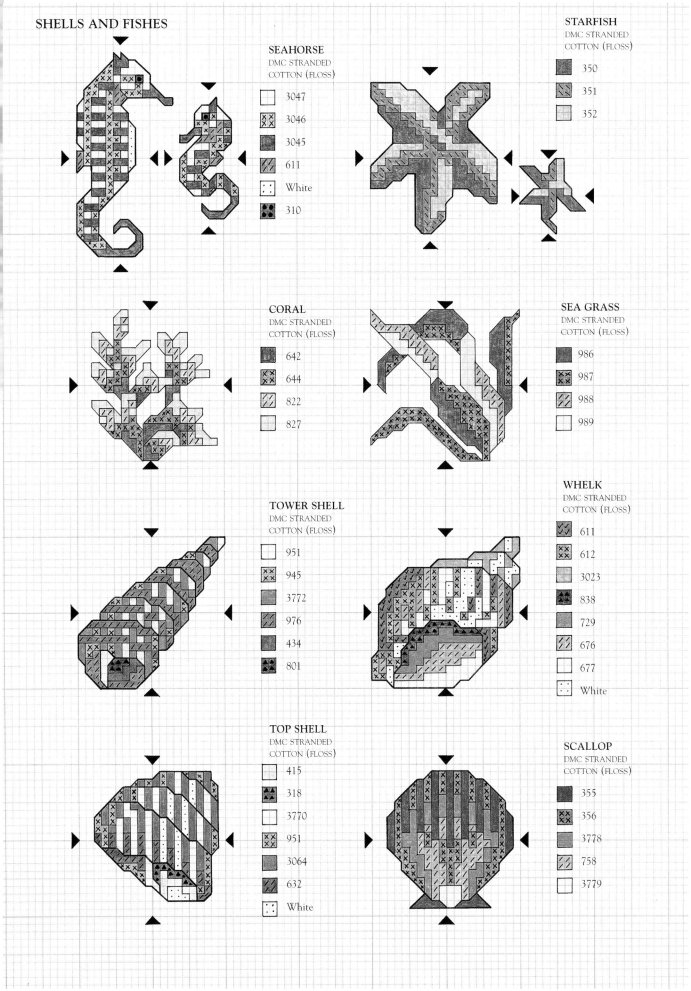

SEAHORSE
DMC STRANDED
COTTON (FLOSS)

☐	3047
☒	3046
▨	3045
▨	611
⊡	White
▨	310

STARFISH
DMC STRANDED
COTTON (FLOSS)

▨	350
▨	351
▨	352

CORAL
DMC STRANDED
COTTON (FLOSS)

▨	642
☒	644
▨	822
▨	827

SEA GRASS
DMC STRANDED
COTTON (FLOSS)

▨	986
☒	987
▨	988
☐	989

TOWER SHELL
DMC STRANDED
COTTON (FLOSS)

☐	951
☒	945
▨	3772
▨	976
▨	434
▲	801

WHELK
DMC STRANDED
COTTON (FLOSS)

✓	611
☒	612
▨	3023
▲	838
▨	729
▨	676
☐	677
⊡	White

TOP SHELL
DMC STRANDED
COTTON (FLOSS)

☐	415
▲	318
☐	3770
☒	951
▨	3064
▨	632
⊡	White

SCALLOP
DMC STRANDED
COTTON (FLOSS)

▨	355
☒	356
▨	3778
▨	758
☐	3779

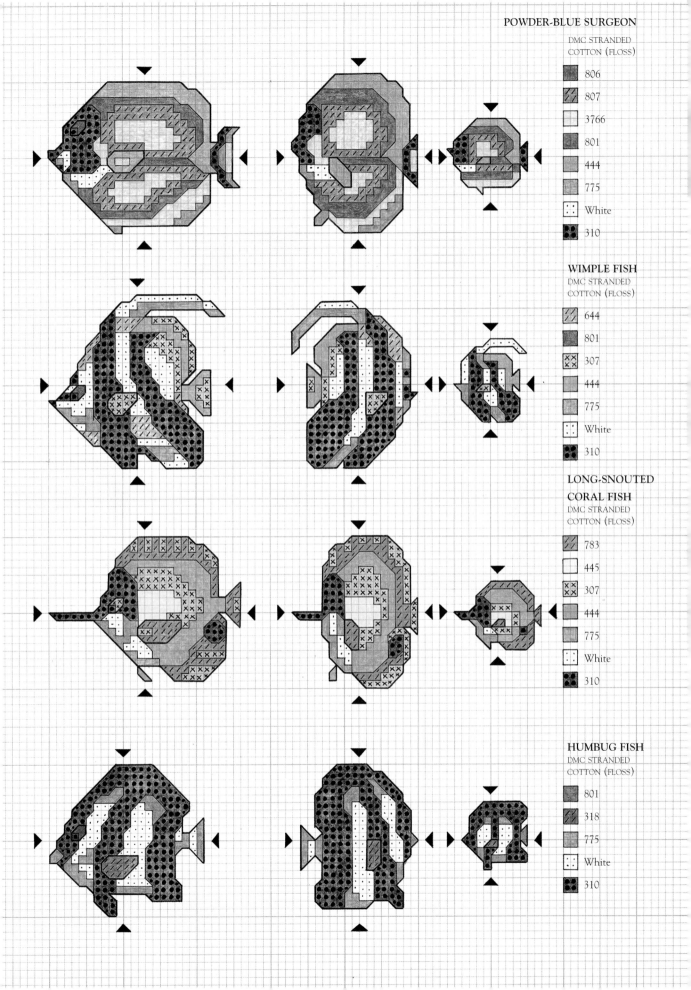

POWDER-BLUE SURGEON

DMC STRANDED
COTTON (FLOSS)

- 806
- 807
- 3766
- 801
- 444
- 775
- White
- 310

WIMPLE FISH

DMC STRANDED
COTTON (FLOSS)

- 644
- 801
- 307
- 444
- 775
- White
- 310

LONG-SNOUTED
CORAL FISH

DMC STRANDED
COTTON (FLOSS)

- 783
- 445
- 307
- 444
- 775
- White
- 310

HUMBUG FISH

DMC STRANDED
COTTON (FLOSS)

- 801
- 318
- 775
- White
- 310

Flower Garland

*This beautiful floral garland bursts with summer flowers in full bloom.
Rich purple and pink fuchsias, bright pink petunias and blue trailing lobelia, combined with lush
green foliage, create a particularly spectacular summer design. As well as stitching the
complete garland on a linen tablecloth, we have repeated the smaller designs on the napkins to
co-ordinate the set. By decorating cushions to match, we're quite ready for
summer picnics and long, lazy lunches in the garden.*

FLOWER GARLAND TABLECLOTH

FINISHED DESIGN SIZES

Floral garland 32 x 32 x 45.5cm (12$^1/_2$ x 12$^1/_2$ x
17$^2/_3$in); floral motif 13cm (5in) square approximately

WHAT YOU WILL NEED

◆ Antique white 20-count Bellana (Zweigart E3256),
   1.40m (1$^1/_2$yd) square
◆ Matching sewing thread

DMC STRANDED COTTON
1 SKEIN

Dark saffron yellow 725; hint of grey 762; coral red 817;
dark coral 349; med coral 350; coral 351; dark mahogany
300; med mahogany 400; dark violet 550; med violet
552; violet 553; dark plum 915; very light rose 3326; med
baby pink 776; dark royal blue 796; dark delft blue 798;
med delft blue 799; delft blue 809; dark leaf green 3345;
very light yellow-green 772

2 SKEINS

White; med ruby 601; light ruby 602; dark sugar pink
603; light baby pink 818; med leaf green 3346; light leaf
green 3347

1 First, read through Techniques, page 9. Neaten
the raw edges of the cloth by pressing up a 1.5cm
($^5/_8$in) turning, and then stitch the hem in place.
Hand embroider to make a decorative hem if you
wish. Refer to the Stitch Guide, pages 11–13, for
how to work the stitches.

2 Work the flower garlands (design A) in two opposite corners, and a floral motif (design B) in each of
the two remaining corners. Work the designs from
the centre outwards.

3 Use three strands of stranded cotton (floss) for the
cross stitch and two strands for the backstitch, over
two threads of evenweave fabric.

4 For backstitch detail use two strands of stranded
cotton (floss) in light ruby 602 for the fuchsia
stamens, and med leaf green 3346 for the lobelia
stems and leaf stems.

FLOWER GARLAND

The summer garden is abundant with lush
flowers in full bloom and delicious fragrant
perfumes which waft on the warm breeze.
Hanging baskets overflowing with colour are
an ideal way of bringing a splash of summer
colour, and these beautiful floral displays
really do make the best of the abundant
summer months.

*This collection is ideal for a summer picnic (from left to
right): Flower Garland Tablecloth, Napkins and Cushion.*

FLOWER GARLAND

DESIGN B

DESIGN C

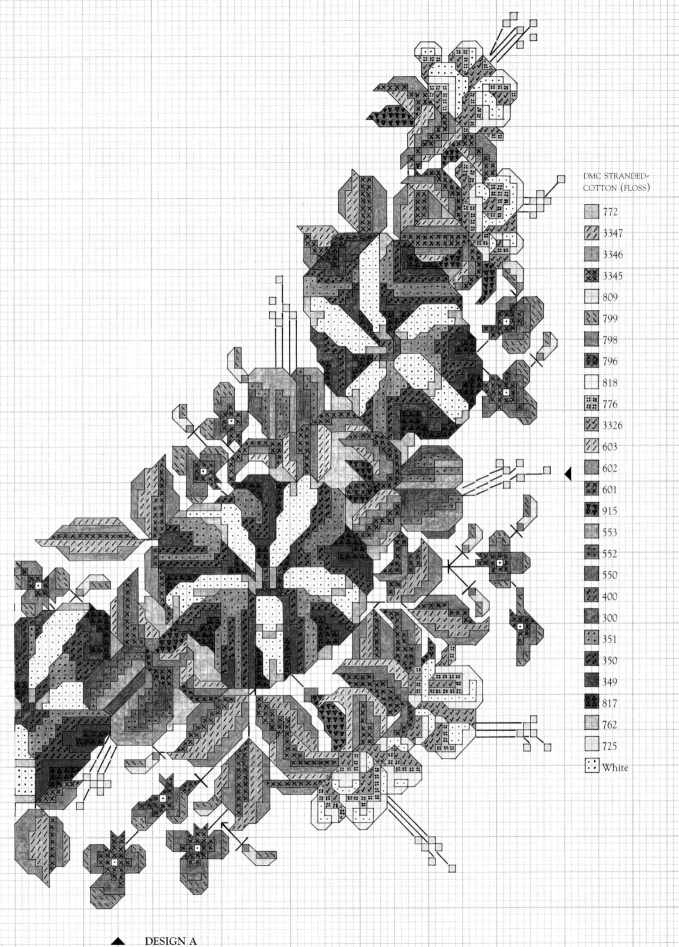

DMC STRANDED-COTTON (FLOSS)

	772
	3347
	3346
	3345
	809
	799
	798
	796
	818
	776
	3326
	603
	602
	601
	915
	553
	552
	550
	400
	300
	351
	350
	349
	817
	762
	725
	White

▲   DESIGN A

FOUR FLOWER GARLAND NAPKINS

FINISHED DESIGN SIZES

Worked over two threads – 7 x 9cm (2³/₄ x 3¹/₂in)
Worked over one thread – 3 x 4cm (1¹/₂ x 1³/₄in)
approximately

WHAT YOU WILL NEED FOR EACH NAPKIN

✦ Antique white 20-count Bellana (Zweigart E3256), 33cm (13in) square
✦ Matching sewing thread

DMC STRANDED COTTON (FLOSS)
1 SKEIN

White; dark saffron yellow 725; dark plum 915; med ruby 601; light ruby 602; dark sugar pink 603; very light rose 3326; med baby pink 776; light baby pink 818; dark royal blue 796; dark delft blue 798; med delft blue 799; delft blue 809; dark leaf green 3345; med leaf green 3346; light leaf green 3347

1 First, read through Techniques, page 9. Neaten the raw edges of each napkin by pressing up a 1cm (¹/₂in) turning, and then stitch the hem in place. Hand embroider to make a decorative hem if you wish. Refer to the Stitch Guide, pages 11–13, for how to work the stitches.
2 Work the small floral motif (design C) at the bottom right corner of each napkin. You can use one strand of stranded cotton (floss) for the cross stitch and backstitch, over one thread of evenweave, or make the motif larger by using two strands of stranded cotton (floss), over two threads of fabric.
3 Work backstitch detail in light ruby 602 for the fuchsia stamens, and med leaf green 3346 for the lobelia stems and leaf stems.

FLOWER GARLAND CUSHION

FINISHED DESIGN SIZE

25cm (9³/₄in) square approximately

WHAT YOU WILL NEED

✦ Sage Green 14-count Aida, (Zweigart E3706), 50cm (20in) square
✦ Cotton fabric for backing and frill, 1m x 115cm (1¹/₈yd x 45in) wide
✦ Zip 30cm (12in) long
✦ Matching sewing thread
✦ Square cushion pad to fit

DMC STRANDED COTTON

Use the list for the flower garland tablecloth, page 64
You will need only one skein of each colour.

1 First, read through Techniques, page 9. Use a soft pencil to mark a 40cm (16in) square in the centre of the Aida fabric, and place each floral garland (design A) 4cm (1³/₄in) below the marked pencil line. Refer to the Stitch Guide, pages 11–13, for how to work the stitches.
2 Use two strands of stranded cotton (floss) for the cross stitch, and one strand for the backstitch. Work backstitch detail in light ruby 602 for the fuchsia stamens, and med leaf green 3346 for the lobelia stems and leaf stems.

TO MAKE UP THE CUSHION

1 For the cushion front, cut away excess fabric along the marked pencil line, leaving an embroidered square with a 1.5cm (⁵/₈in) seam allowance.
2 For the cushion back, cut two pieces of cotton fabric 21.5 x 40cm (8¹/₂ x 16in). With right sides facing, pin and tack (baste) pieces together along one long edge, then stitch 5cm (2in) in from both ends leaving a gap at the centre. Press seam open and insert zip, following the instructions for the floral patchwork cushions on page 34.
3 To complete, follow making up steps 4 and 5 for the floral cushion, page 34, then insert a square cushion pad to fit.

Work this fuschia and lobelia motif over one or two threads of fabric, using one or two strands of cotton (floss), to create a larger or smaller decoration for the Flower Garland Napkins.

Foxglove Collection

These lofty wildflowers are a wonderful sight in the hedgerows in the late summer months;
and, along with hollyhocks, must be everyone's idea of a typical cottage garden flower.
Our interpretations of wild foxgloves make the most of their slender elegance by applying them to
bell-pull, draft excluder and finger plate. Delicate bell-shaped flowers are beautifully worked in rich
shades of mauves and violets.

FOXGLOVE BELL PULL

FINISHED DESIGN SIZE
11 x 47 cm (4^{1}/4 x 18^{1}/2 in) approximately

WHAT YOU WILL NEED
- White 14-count Aida (Zweigart E3706), 28 x 66cm (11 x 26in)
- Cotton backing fabric, 20 x 90cm (^{1}/4 yd x 36in) wide
- Bell pull hanging rod, 18cm (7in) long
- Contrast furnishing braid, 1.5m (1^{5}/8 yd)
- Matching sewing thread

DMC STRANDED COTTON (FLOSS)
1 SKEIN
Black 310; white; light mauve 3609; med mauve 3608; dark mauve 3607; light plum 718; med plum 917; dark plum 915; very dark violet 327; dark violet 550; light baby pink 818; flesh 754; very light leaf green 3348; light leaf green 3347; med leaf green 3346; dark leaf green 3345; very dark brown 938; dark topaz 781; light yellow-green 772; med mahogany 400; light mahogany 301; med golden-green 581; dark golden green 580; light forest green 989; light brass 834; light tangerine 742; med grey 648; dark antique gold 370; light tan 437; brown 433

1 First, read through Techniques, page 9. The length of the bell pull hanging rod determines the width of the fabric. The hanging rod used here allows for a 13cm (5in) wide strip. Purchase the rods before you start working the design to ensure that they will be wide enough.

2 Refer to the Stitch Guide, pages 11–13, for how to work the stitches, and then work the design from the centre outwards, allowing plenty of excess fabric around the edges.

3 Use two strands of stranded cotton (floss) for the cross stitch.

4 Work backstitch detail using two strands of stranded cotton (floss) in dark leaf green 3345 for the grass and foxglove seed heads. Use one strand in black 310 to outline the bee's body, wings and legs, and very dark brown 938 to outline the butterflies. When you have completed the stitching, press.

TO MAKE THE BELL PULL
1 Mark the correct width and length of the bell pull on to the fabric with tacking (basting) lines. Cut the fabric adding 1.5cm (^{5}/8 in) along both long and diagonal edges, and 5cm (2in) at the top edge. Press turnings in place and mitre all corners (fig 27). Cut

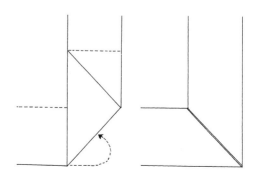

Fig 27: Mitred corners

the backing fabric to the same size, but add a 1.5cm (⁵/₈in) turning all the way round.

2 Hand stitch furnishing braid around both long and diagonal edges of the embroidered fabric. Position the hanging rod at the top of the strip, on the wrong side under the fold of the turnings. Hand stitch the turning in place along the outer edges, then finish by stitching backing fabric into place.

DRAUGHT EXCLUDER

FINISHED DESIGN SIZE
18 x 79cm (7 x 31in), approximately

WHAT YOU WILL NEED
- ◆ Summer Khaki 16-count Aida (E3251), 38 x 110cm (15 x 43in)
- ◆ Cotton backing fabric, 30cm x 115cm (³/₈yd x 45in) wide
- ◆ Heavyweight cotton fabric for lining, 60 x 115cm (³/₄yd x 45in) wide
- ◆ Rice or wadding (batting) for filling
- ◆ Furnishing braid, 2.3m (2¹/₂yd)
- ◆ Matching sewing thread

DMC STRANDED COTTON (FLOSS)
Use the list for the foxglove bell pull; but you will need two skeins each of light mauve 3609; light plum 718; dark violet 550; med leaf green 3346 and dark leaf green 3345

1 First, read through the instructions given in the Techniques on page 9, and prepare your fabric. Refer to the Stitch Guide, pages 11–13, for how to work the stitches, and work the design from the centre outwards.

2 Use four strands of stranded cotton (floss) for the cross stitch, working over two blocks of Aida.

3 Work backstitch detail over two blocks of Aida. Use four strands of stranded cotton (floss) in dark leaf green 3345 for the grass and foxglove seed heads. Use two strands in black 310 to outline the bees body, wings and legs, and very dark brown 938 to outline the butterflies.

4 When the embroidery is complete, use a soft pencil to draw a rectangle all around the design, measuring 2.5cm (1in) from the top, bottom and widest parts. Cut away excess fabric along these lines. Cut one piece of backing fabric and two pieces of cotton lining to the same size.

The Foxglove Collection: Draught Excluder, Bell Pull and Door Finger-plate

5 With right sides facing, place the front and back pieces together, pin, tack (baste) and stitch around the two long edges and one short edge, leaving the remaining short edge open. Turn fabric through to right side. Repeat for the lining fabric.

6 Fill the lining with rice or wadding (batting), then secure the gap with slipstitch. Put the filled lining inside the embroidered tube, then secure the gap with slipstitch. Slipstitch the furnishing braid around the seam line on the outer edge.

DOOR FINGER-PLATE

FINISHED DESIGN SIZE
6 x 23.5cm (2¹/₄ x 9¹/₄in)

WHAT YOU WILL NEED
- ◆ White 27-count Linda (Zweigart E1235), 21 x 39cm (8¹/₄ x 15¹/₄in)
- ◆ Perspex finger plate fitting

DMC STRANDED COTTON (FLOSS)
Use the list for the foxglove bell pull

1 Follow step 1 for the foxglove draught excluder.

2 Use one strand of stranded cotton (floss) for the cross stitch and backstitch.

3 Work backstitch detail in dark leaf green 3345 for the grass and foxglove seed heads; in black 310 to outline the bee's body, wings and legs; and very dark brown 938 to outline the butterflies.

4 Finally, to mount the completed embroidery into the finger-plate, follow the manufacturer's instructions.

FOXGLOVES
Although the plant is poisonous, foxglove is used to manufacture the drug digitalis, an important treatment for heart complaints. Its Anglo-Saxon name, which translates as 'small bells' and 'little folk', explains the association with fairies. It was also thought that some bad fairies gave the flowers to the foxes to wear on their paws so that they could creep silently on their prey.

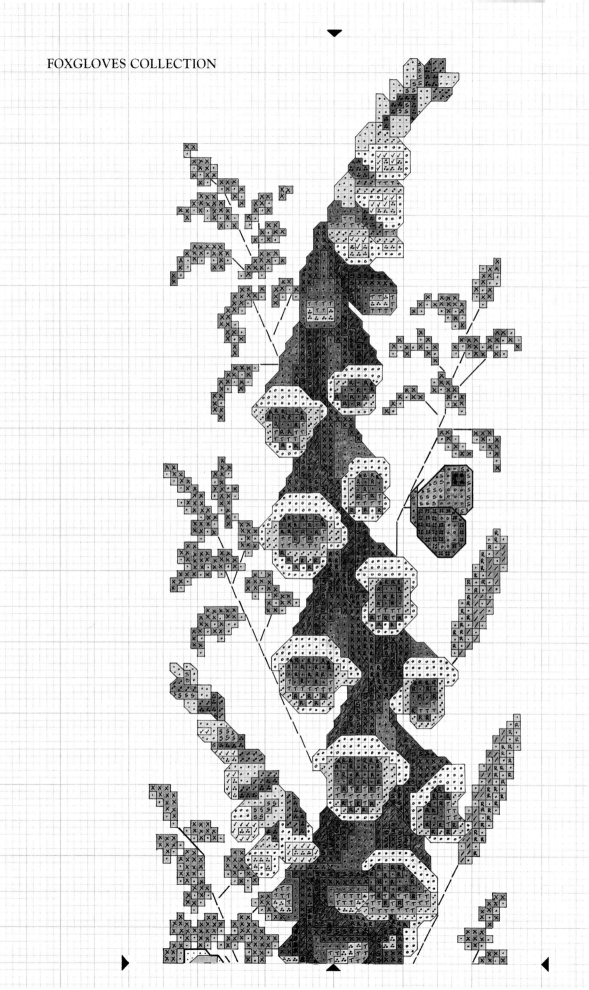

DMC STRANDED
COTTON (FLOSS)

433	
437	
370	
648	
742	
834	
989	
580	
581	
301	
400	
772	
781	
938	
3345	
3346	
3347	
3348	
754	
818	
550	
327	
915	
917	
718	
3607	
3608	
3609	
White	
310	

AUTUMN

Autumn is a magical season, with gardens and countryside decked out in golden browns, rusts and reds, a golden carpet of crunchy leaves coating the ground.

Our projects celebrating autumn include 'Autumn Hedgehog' (opposite), worked in embroidery threads and silk ribbon embroidery, in search of food before finding a nice cosy place to hibernate for the winter; and the 'Wild Mushroom' collection (page 93), used with desk accessories for a study – ideal for the man of the house. 'Mice, Brambles and Berries' is a super design of scampering mice in search of shiny blackberries, worked using tiny glass beads to make them really sparkle (page 79). The beautiful 'Autumn Leaves' (page 90), with its crispy golden leaves, shiny brown conkers and bright green acorns, makes a colourful cushion and pincushion. The biggest and most ambitious project in the book, on page 84, is the 'Barn Owl'. This majestic bird sits proudly amongst the autumn foliage and fungus, ready to swoop on anything that moves. Our final autumnal project is an unusual abstract of a female adder, slithering through the undergrowth and fallen autumn leaves (page 97).

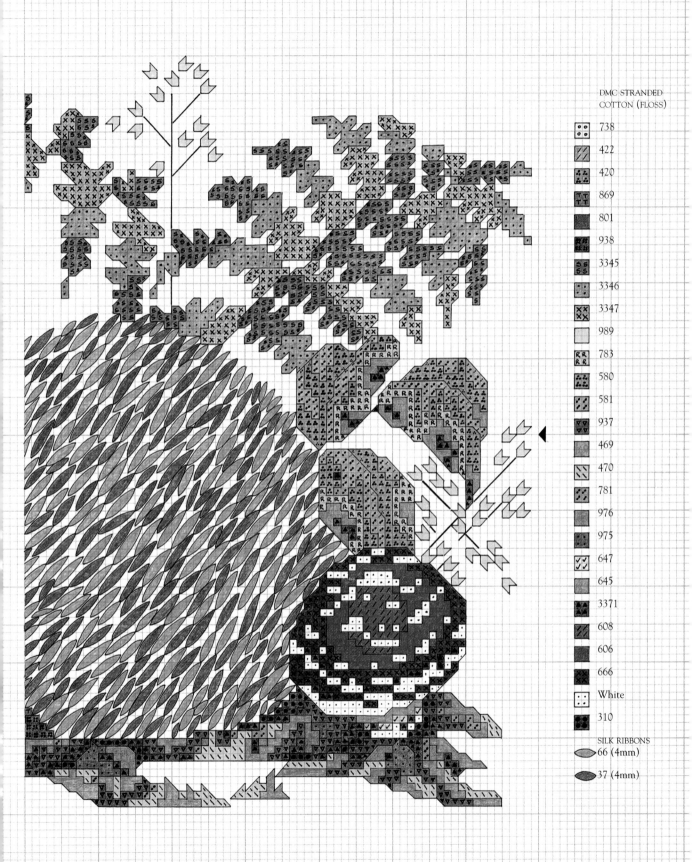

DMC·STRANDED
COTTON (FLOSS)

• • / • •	738
/ /	422
•• ••	420
T T / T T	869
▨	801
▨	938
S S / S S	3345
•• / ••	3346
X X / X X	3347
	989
R R / R R	783
•• ••	580
•• ••	581
▽ / ▽	937
	469
⧄	470
•• ••	781
	976
•• ••	975
✓✓ / ✓✓	647
	645
▲▲ / ▲▲	3371
/ /	608
▨	606
▨	666
•• ••	White
▨	310

SILK RIBBONS

⬭	66 (4mm)
⬮	37 (4mm)

Autumn Hedgehog

*Hedgehogs are a familiar autumn sight, scurrying about
hedgerows, roadsides and gardens in search of slugs and snails, fruits and fungus
or scraps left out for them.
Our autumnal picture is rich with colour and texture, using silk ribbon
embroidery for the hedgehog's prickly spines, and smooth cross stitch for the distinctive
red and white fly agaric mushrooms and autumn foliage.*

FINISHED DESIGN SIZE
19 x 26.5cm (7^1/$_2$ x 10^1/$_2$ in) approximately

WHAT YOU WILL NEED
✦ Parchment 14-count Aida (Zweigart E3706),
38 x 46cm (15 x 18in)

DMC STRANDED COTTON (FLOSS)
1 SKEIN
Black 310; white; Christmas red 666; bright orange-red
606; bright orange 608; brown-black 3371; dark smoke
grey 645; dark grey 647; chestnut brown 975; med soft
orange 976; dark topaz 781; med moss green 470; dark
moss green 469; med avocado green 937; med golden
green 581; dark golden green 580; light topaz 783; light
forest green 989; light leaf green 3347; med leaf green
3346; dark leaf green 3345; very dark brown 938; med
brown 801; dark caramel 869; med caramel 420; light
caramel 422 and dark cream 738.

RIBBON DESIGNS SILK RIBBONS
4mm wide: light brown (colour 66), 4m (4^3/$_8$ yd); brown
(colour 37), 4m (4^3/$_8$ yd)

1 First, read through Techniques, page 9, and
prepare your fabric. Refer to the Stitch Guide, pages
11–13, for how to work the stitches, and work the
design from the centre outwards.
2 Work all the cross stitch areas first, then work any
backstitch detail, and finally fill in the areas of silk
ribbon embroidery.
3 Use two strands of stranded cotton (floss) for the
cross stitch, and one strand for the backstitch.

4 Work the backstitch detail in black 310 for the
hedgehog's nose and eye, and light forest green 989
for the grass stems. Use brown-black 3371 for
working the backstitch detail for the toadstool gills
and frill, and also to outline the snail's body, shell
and antennae.
5 Work the hedgehog spines in silk ribbon
embroidery. The colours and widths of ribbons used
are indicated on the colour key.
6 Refer to Mounting and Framing, page 10, for how
to complete your picture.

HEDGEHOG
Hedgehogs, or 'urchins', are often seen in
gardens and hedgerows in late autumn before
they hibernate for winter. These prickly
creatures have sparse, course hair on their
head and belly, and their backs are covered
with about 6000 spines. They have very poor
eyesight, but their acute hearing and sense of
smell helps them to feed at night on earth-
worms, beetles, caterpillars, spiders and slugs.
After gorging themselves they sleep it off
during the day, curled up in a nest of leaves.

Mice, Brambles and Berries

*Mischievous mice running amongst the hedgerow, searching for blackberries to feast on,
embellish this charming waistcoat. Black fabric contrasts dramatically with the red, rust and green
of the mice and leaves, and also emphasises the delicate pink-tinged flower petals.
Added sparkle and texture is created by the purple beads used to work the juicy blackberries,
making them look good enough to eat! The buttons and brooch are themselves miniature works of
art, worked on fine silk gauze with 40 threads to 1in!*

WAISTCOAT

FINISHED DESIGN SIZE
11 x 30.5cm (4¹/₄ x 12in) approximately

WHAT YOU WILL NEED
- ✦ Purchased pattern for waistcoat
- ✦ Black 27-count Linda (Zweigart E1235), or other linen or blockweave fabric (refer to pattern for fabric requirements)
- ✦ Fabric for backing and lining (refer to pattern for fabric requirements)
- ✦ Buttons (refer to pattern for number of buttons required)
- ✦ Matching sewing thread

DMC STRANDED COTTON
1 SKEIN
Black 310; white; light baby pink 818; med baby pink 776; med yellow 743; pale yellow 745; very dark brown 938; dark orange-spice 720; med orange-spice 721; light topaz 783; med avocado green 937; bronze 730; dark yellow-green 732; med yellow-green 733; dark mahogany 300; peach 353; brown 433; very dark tan 434; dark tan 435; med tan 436; light tan 437; dark cream 738 and med cream 739; (also, if you work the blackberries in French knots, dark violet 550 and very dark violet 327)

The blackberries can either be worked using small glass beads or French knots. The colour key on the chart lists the shade codes for both.

MILL HILL BEADS
Frosted glass beads – 1 pack: lavender 62047; royal purple 62042; black 62014

1 Lay the pattern pieces for the waistcoat fronts on to the fabric and tack (baste) around their shapes with sewing thread. You may find it easier to stitch the designs on to the fabric before cutting out the waistcoat fronts.

2 Read through Techniques, page 9. Refer to the Stitch Guide, pages 11–13, for how to work the stitches and attach beads, and work the design from the centre outwards.

3 Use two strands of stranded cotton (floss) for the cross stitch and French knots, and one strand for the backstitch. Work cross stitch and backstitch over two threads.

4 Work backstitch detail in very dark brown 938 for the mice's noses and ears, and the flower petals. Use a small black bead or a French knot for each eye.

5 The blackberries can be worked in either glass beads (see page 80) or French knots (below).

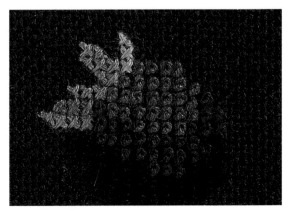

HEDGEROW BERRIES

For just a few precious weeks each summer, wonderful hedgerow fruits ripen and become a delicious treat for both animals and humans. Blackberries have to be eaten as soon as possible after picking, on their own with cream or ice-cream, or made into jams, jellies, delicious summer puddings, or homemade wine.

To repeat the design on both sides of the waistcoat, the chart needs to be reversed. This can be done by photocopying the chart in reverse.

TO MAKE UP THE WAISTCOAT

Make the waistcoat following the instructions for the purchased paper pattern. Add buttons which complement the colours of the design, or add decorative embroidered buttons. We have used small gilt buttons, but plastic cover buttons could also be used. To make your waistcoat really special, pick out a colour from the completed embroidered design, and chose a lining fabric to match. Use this to make the waistcoat lining and to make co-ordinating covered buttons.

BUTTONS AND BROOCH

FINISHED DESIGN SIZE
Buttons – 13mm ($^5/_8$ in) approximately; brooch – 30 x 40mm ($1^1/_4$ x $1^3/_4$ in) approximately

WHAT YOU WILL NEED
✦ Fine silk gauze, 40-count, to fit size of button or brooch
✦ Buttons and brooch
All available from Elizabeth R Anderson (see Stockists, page 127)

DMC STRANDED COTTON (FLOSS)
1 SKEIN
Buttons – white; light baby pink 818; med baby pink 776; med yellow 743; pale yellow 745; very dark brown 938; dark orange-spice 720; med orange-spice 721; light topaz 783; bronze 730; dark yellow-green 732; med yellow-green 733. **Brooch** – black 310; white; light baby pink 818; med baby pink 776; med yellow 743; pale yellow 745; very dark brown 938; dark orange-spice 720; med orange-spice 721; light topaz 783; bronze 730; dark yellow-green 732; med yellow-green 733; peach 353; brown 433; very dark tan 434; dark tan 435; med tan 436; light tan 437; dark cream 738; med cream 739; dark violet 550; very dark violet 327

1 Follow step 2 for the waistcoat.
2 Because the silk gauze is so fine, the designs have to be stitched in half cross stitch, using one strand of stranded cotton (floss).
3 To complete your buttons and brooch, follow the manufacturer's instructions.

Mice, Brambles and Berries Button and Brooch

MICE, BRAMBLES AND BERRIES

BUTTONS

BROOCH

WAISTCOAT FRONTS (TOP)

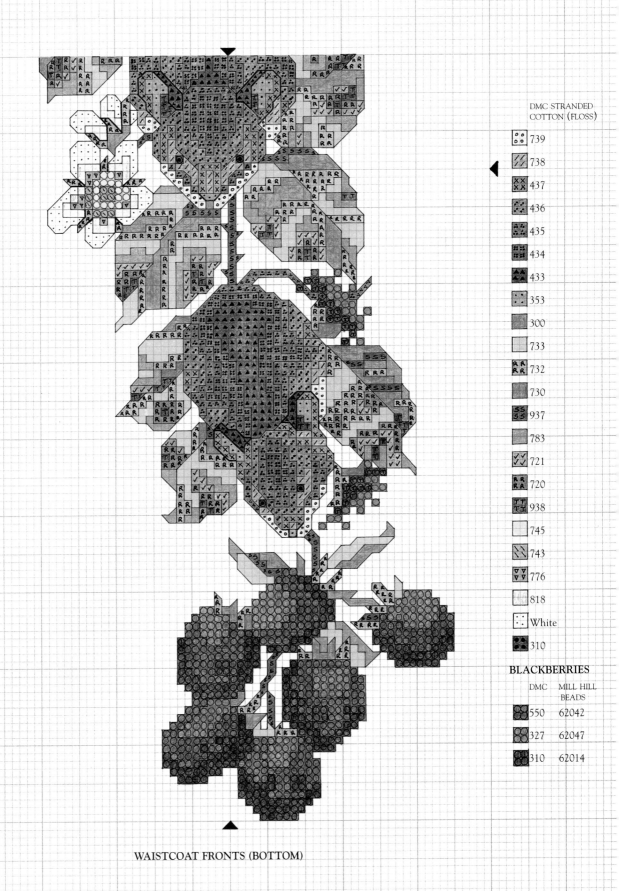

DMC STRANDED
COTTON (FLOSS)

○○	739
╱╱	738
✗✗	437
∴∴	436
▲▲	435
✦✦	434
▲▲	433
∵∵	353
	300
	733
RR RR	732
	730
SS SS	937
	783
✓✓	721
RR RR	720
TT TT	938
	745
╲╲	743
▽▽ ▽▽	776
	818
∷	White
✦✦	310

BLACKBERRIES

	DMC	MILL HILL BEADS
⊛⊛	550	62042
⊛⊛	327	62047
⊛⊛	310	62014

WAISTCOAT FRONTS (BOTTOM)

Barn Owl

The barn owl must be one of the most beautiful and well known of the owl family.
This handsome bird is the largest and most ambitious project in the book, worked completely
in cross stitch and three-quarter stitch with no backstitch detail.
The intricate detailing of the owl's feathers and the lush foliage is achieved by using over thirty
different shades of greens, golden browns and rusts, set against a khaki background.

FINISHED DESIGN SIZE
30.5 x 37cm (12 x 14¹/₂ in) approximately

WHAT YOU WILL NEED
◆ Khaki 14-count Aida (Zweigart E3706),
50 x 56cm (20 x 22in)

DMC STRANDED COTTON
1 SKEIN
Black 310; light grey-brown 3024; dark grey-brown 3022; donkey brown 3787; very dark brown 938; med brown 801; chestnut brown 975; light mahogany 301; med topaz 782; light tangerine 742; off white 746; light old gold 676; dark old gold 680; med steel grey 414; light ash grey 415; light mink 842; chocolate brown 839; med tangerine 741; dark topaz 781; med avocado green 937; dark moss green 469; med moss green 470; very dark salmon 347; med leaf green 3346; light leaf green 3347; med bottle green 319; dark sage green 367; light sage green 368; hint of green 369; med old gold 729; very dark topaz 780; brown 433; dark tan 435

2 SKEINS
White

1 First, read through Techniques, page 9, and prepare your fabric. Refer to the Stitch Guide, pages 11–13, for how to work the stitches, and work the design from the centre outwards.
2 Work the owl first, followed by the ferns and autumn foliage.

3 Use two strands of stranded cotton (floss) for the cross stitch.
4 Refer to Mounting and Framing, page 10, for how to complete your picture.

BARN OWLS
These beautiful pale-coloured birds have a distinctive heart-shaped face with large forward facing eyes and a hooked bill. The upper body is golden-buff with fine grey speckles, tapering down to long legs with powerful claws. The heart-shaped face looks pretty but it is also very important as sound reflects off the flat face and into the ears, helping the owl to hear the tiniest of noises. In the winter months these nocturnal creatures often hunt by day for small rodents scurrying along the ground, and the very low, slow, noiseless flight enables them to swoop on their unsuspecting prey.

BARN OWL

DMC STRANDED
COTTON (FLOSS)

	435
	433
	780
	729
	369
	368
	367
	319
	3347
	3346
	347
	470
	469
	937
	781
	741
	839
	842
	415
	414
	680
	676
	746
	742
	782
	301
	975
	801
	938
	3787
	3022
	3024
	White
	310

BARN OWL

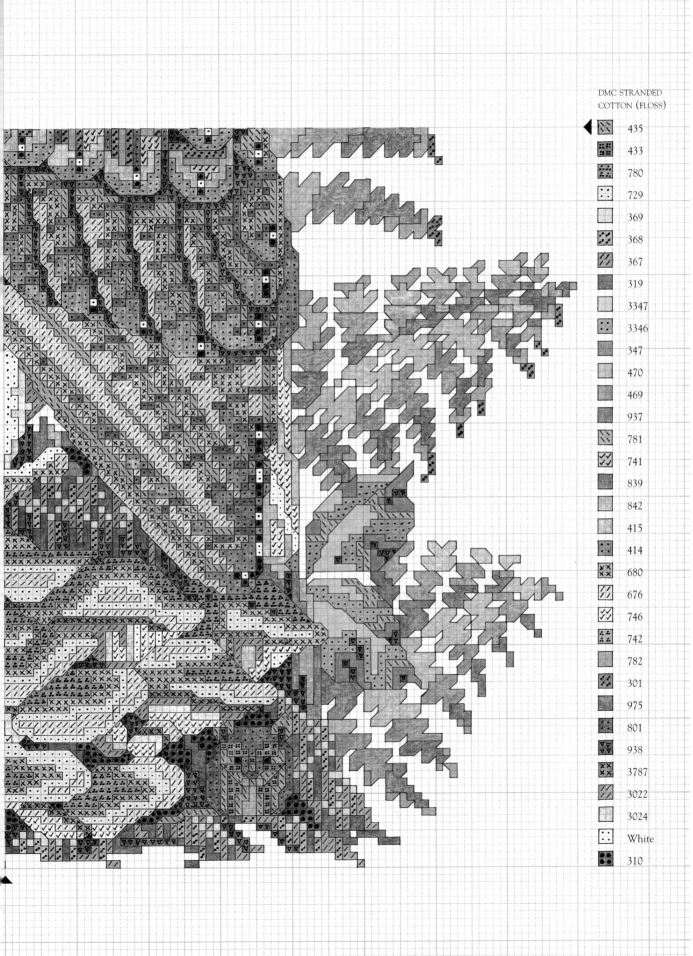

DMC STRANDED
COTTON (FLOSS)

◣	435
	433
	780
	729
	369
	368
	367
	319
	3347
	3346
	347
	470
	469
	937
	781
	741
	839
	842
	415
	414
	680
	676
	746
	742
	782
	301
	975
	801
	938
	3787
	3022
	3024
	White
	310

Autumn Leaves

The warm colours of autumn are captured in this design – shiny dark brown conkers and bright green acorns amongst the rich reds, oranges and rusts of the crisp autumn leaves. The small design on the pincushion is repeated four times in the central panel of the cushion, which has a richly worked border around the edge and decorative trim echoing the colours of the design.

PINCUSHION

FINISHED DESIGN SIZE
9cm (3¹/₂ in) square approximately

WHAT YOU WILL NEED
- Khaki 14-count Aida (Zweigart E3706), 23cm (9in) square
- Scrap of felt for backing
- Polyester wadding (batting) for filling
- Furnishing braid, 50cm (⁵/₈ yd)
- Matching sewing thread

DMC STRANDED COTTON (FLOSS)
Use the list of stranded cotton (floss) for the autumn leaves cushion, but omit the last four shades of: chestnut brown 975; dark orange-spice 720; med tangerine 741; light tangerine 742

1 Follow step 1 for the autumn leaves cushion.
2 Use two strands of stranded cotton (floss) for the cross stitch and work only the smaller motif, without the border, from the chart on page 92.
3 Cut away excess fabric to within 2.5cm (1in) of the finished design. Cut a piece of felt to the same size. Place the pieces with right sides together and machine stitch 1.5cm (5/8in) from the outer edge, leaving a 9cm (3 1/2in) gap for turning.
4 Turn the pincushion through to the right side, stuff with wadding (batting) and slipstitch the gap.
5 Slipstitch furnishing braid round the edge.

CUSHION

FINISHED DESIGN SIZE
37cm (14¹/₂ in) square approximately

WHAT YOU WILL NEED
- Black 14-count Aida (Zweigart E3706), 57cm (22¹/₂in) square
- Cotton fabric for backing, 40 x 90cm (¹/₂ yd x 36in) wide
- 30cm (12in) zip
- Thick furnishing braid, 1.8m (2yd)
- Matching sewing thread
- Square cushion-pad to fit

DMC STRANDED COTTON (FLOSS)
1 SKEIN
Med brown 801; brown 433; very dark tan 434; med tan 436; very light moss green 472; dark moss green 469; med avocado green 937; dark saffron yellow 725; very dark leaf green 895; dark leaf green 3345; med leaf green 3346; very dark golden brown 829; dark golden brown 830; med golden brown 831; dark brass 832; med brass 833; light brass 834; dark old gold 680; dark rust 918; med rust 919; dark copper 920; med copper 921; brown-black 3371; bright orange-red 606; very dark topaz 780; med topaz 782; med old gold 729; med golden green 581; chestnut brown 975; dark orange-spice 720; med tangerine 741; light tangerine 742

1 First, read through Techniques, page 9, and prepare your fabric. Refer to the Stitch Guide, pages 11–13, for how to work the stitches.

Autumn Leaves Cushion (left) and Pincushion (right) capture the glowing colours of autumn.

2 The design chart shows one quarter of the design, and has to be repeated four times. Work the first section of the cushion from the centre outwards, then match points A and B on the chart to complete the design by stitching the three remaining sections.

3 Use two strands of stranded cotton (floss) for the cross stitch.

TO MAKE UP THE CUSHION

1 For the cushion front, cut away excess fabric to within 5cm (2in) of the finished design, to allow for a 1.5cm (⁵/₈ in) seam allowance.

2 For the cushion back, cut two pieces of cotton fabric 22.5 x 42cm (8³/₄ x 16¹/₂ in). With right sides facing, pin and tack (baste) the pieces together along one long edge, then stitch 6cm (2¹/₄ in) in from both ends leaving a gap at the centre. Neaten both long edges, then press the seam open and insert the zip following the instructions for the floral patchwork cushion, page 34.

3 To complete, follow making up step 5 for the floral patchwork cushion, page 34.

4 Slipstitch the thick furnishing braid around the edge.

AUTUMN LEAVES

DMC STRANDED
COTTON (FLOSS)

801		937		830		918		780			
433		725		831		919		782			
434		895		832		920		729		741	
436		3345		833		921		581		742	
472		3346		834		3371		975			
469		829		680		606		720			

Wild Mushroom Study

These unusual wild mushroom designs are worked in cross stitch, three-quarter cross and backstitch detail. Shaggy ink cap, chanterelle, field mushroom and fairy ring champignon here represent the many fascinating varieties of wild mushrooms to be found in field and forest. Our stunning picture uses all four, whilst individual designs have been used for desk accessories, such as the fairy ring champignon paperweight. The warm colours of the chanterelle are complemented by the rich wooden trinket box, and the shaggy ink cap looks wonderful on the unusual address book.

WILD MUSHROOM PICTURE

FINISHED DESIGN SIZE
7.5 x 30.5cm (3 x 12in) approximately

WHAT YOU WILL NEED
✦ Cream 14-count Aida (Zweigart E3706), 28 x 50cm (11 x 20in)

DMC STRANDED COTTON (FLOSS)
1 SKEIN

Fairy-ring champignon – med flesh 951; light leaf green 3347; med leaf green 3346; very dark brown 938; light mahogany 301; med soft orange 976; soft orange 977; light old gold 676; chocolate brown 839; med mink 841.

Field mushroom – white; light leaf green 3347; med leaf green 3346; very dark brown 938; dark mink 840; med mink 841; light mink 842; very light pink-beige 543; very dark pink-brown 632; light pink-brown 3064; light pink-beige 3774.

Shaggy ink cap – white; light leaf green 3347; med leaf green 3346; very dark brown 938; dark donkey brown 3021; donkey brown 3787; dark grey-brown 3022; very dark tan 434; med caramel 420; med tan 436; light tan 437; light caramel 422.

Chanterelle – white; light leaf green 3347; med leaf green 3346; very dark brown 938; med topaz 782; light topaz 783; dark saffron yellow 725; med mink 841; light yellow 744

1 First, read through Techniques, page 9, and prepare your fabric. Refer to the Stitch Guide, pages 11–13, for how to work the stitches, and work the design from the centre outwards.

2 Use two strands of stranded cotton (floss) for the cross stitch, and one strand for the backstitch. Work backstitch detail in very dark brown 938, to define the parts of the stalks and gills on the underparts of the chanterelle, fairy-ring champignon and field mushroom and the scales of the shaggy ink cap.

3 Refer to Mounting and Framing, page 10, for how to complete your picture.

WILD MUSHROOMS
Woodland and field mushrooms can both be transformed into a feast of seasonal dishes. The shaggy ink cap, edible when young, can be found in lawns, compost heaps and wastelands; the distinctive funnel shaped chanterelle, with its velvety undulating surface folds has a fruity smell which is irresistible when they are fried; the edible field mushroom, the most familiar and in plentiful supply in supermarkets, is rather tasteless in comparison. However, in britain, wild fungi are usually left for mice and insects to feed on.

Above: *Wild Mushroom Picture*
Opposite: *Trinket Box, Address Book and Paperweight*

SHAGGY INK CAP ADDRESS BOOK

FINISHED DESIGN SIZE
7.5cm (3in) square approximately

WHAT YOU WILL NEED
✦ Cream 14-count Aida (Zweigart E3706),
23cm (9in) square

DMC STRANDED COTTON (FLOSS)
Use the list for the wild mushroom picture

1 Follow step 1 for the wild mushroom picture.
2 Use two strands of stranded cotton (floss) for the cross stitch, and one strand for the backstitch. Work backstitch detail in very dark brown 938 to define the scales on the cap of the mushroom and parts of the stalks.
3 To complete your address book, follow the manufacturer's instructions.

FAIRY-RING CHAMPIGNON PAPERWEIGHT

FINISHED DESIGN SIZE
7.5cm (3in) square approximately

WHAT YOU WILL NEED
✦ Cream 14-count Aida (Zweigart E3706),
23cm (9in) square

DMC STRANDED COTTON (FLOSS)
Use the list for the wild mushroom picture

1 Follow step 1 for the wild mushroom picture.
2 Use two strands of stranded cotton (floss) for the cross stitch, and one strand for the backstitch. Work backstitch detail in very dark brown 938 to define the gills on the underpart of the mushroom and parts of the stalks.
3 To complete your paperweight, follow the manufacturer's instructions.

CHANTERELLE TRINKET BOX

FINISHED DESIGN SIZE
7.5cm (3in) square approximately

WHAT YOU WILL NEED
✦ Cream 14-count Aida (Zweigart E3706),
23cm (9in) square

DMC STRANDED COTTON (FLOSS)
Use the list for the wild mushroom picture

1 Follow step 1 for the wild mushroom picture.
2 Use two strands of stranded cotton (floss) for the cross stitch, and one strand for the backstitch. Work backstitch detail in very dark brown 938, to define the gills on the underparts of the mushrooms.
3 To complete your trinket box follow the manufacturer's instructions.

WILD MUSHROOM STUDY

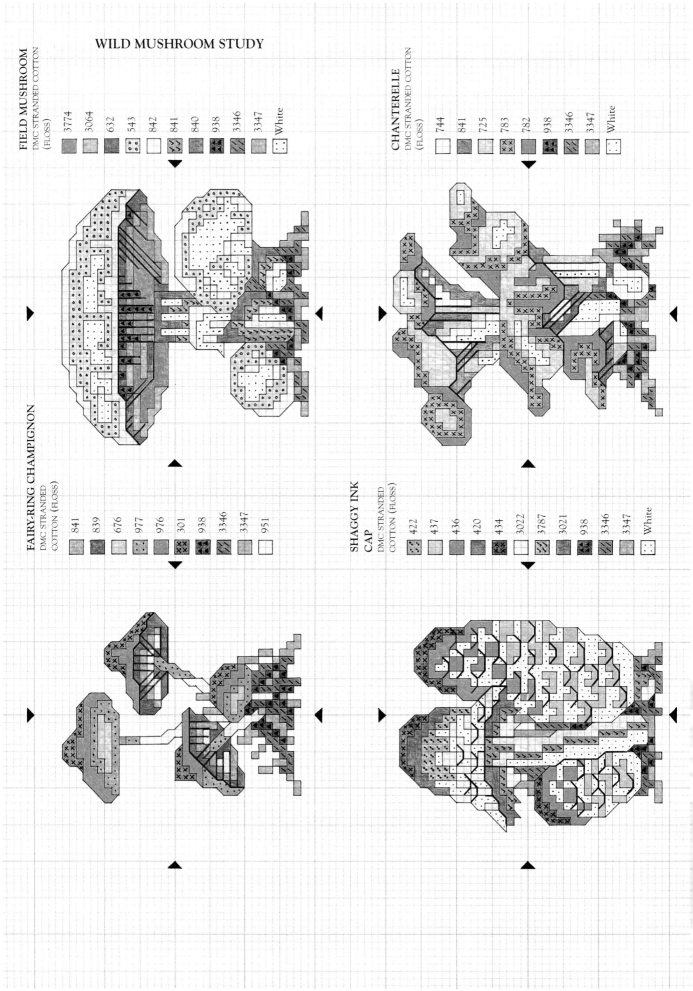

FIELD MUSHROOM
DMC STRANDED COTTON
(FLOSS)

- 3774
- 3064
- 632
- 543
- 842
- 841
- 840
- 938
- 3346
- 3347
- White

FAIRY-RING CHAMPIGNON
DMC STRANDED
COTTON (FLOSS)

- 841
- 839
- 676
- 977
- 976
- 301
- 938
- 3346
- 3347
- 951

CHANTERELLE
DMC STRANDED COTTON
(FLOSS)

- 744
- 841
- 725
- 783
- 782
- 938
- 3346
- 3347
- White

SHAGGY INK CAP
DMC STRANDED
COTTON (FLOSS)

- 422
- 437
- 436
- 420
- 434
- 3022
- 3787
- 3021
- 938
- 3346
- 3347
- White

Adder and Autumn Leaves

*Look very closely at the pile of tumbled autumn leaves and you'll soon be aware of
the sinuous adder, subtly blending with her background. Her distinctive black
zig-zag pattern and chocolate brown colouring merges with the deep fiery red, rust, flame orange
and deep yellow leaves – a perfect match. The design is worked in whole cross stitches
throughout, with no backstitch detailing; in stranded cotton (floss) for the cushion,
and tapestry wool (yarn) for the firescreen.*

ADDER FIRESCREEN

FINISHED DESIGN SIZE
38 x 50cm (15 x 20in) approximately

WHAT YOU WILL NEED
✦ White 10-count single thread interlock canvas
(Zweigart E604A), 56 x 68cm (22 x 27in)

DMC TAPESTRY WOOL (YARN)
1 SKEIN
White; med caramel 7846; light caramel 7739; pale yellow 7078; light yellow 7727; dark saffron yellow 7725; light topaz 7484; med topaz 7782; dark topaz 7781; very dark topaz 7508; soft orange 7919; med soft orange 7922; dark ecru 7520; light brown-beige 7521; med brown-beige 7519; dark brown-beige 7518; med brown 7479; very deep avocado green 7359; dark moss green 7364; dark brick red 7447; bright orange-red 7606

2 SKEINS
Black; brown-black 7938; dark caramel 7845; chestnut brown 7700; light yellow-green 7678; med yellow-green 7677; dark yellow-green 7676; bronze 7573

Border edging – 13 skeins: very deep avocado green 7359

1 First, read through Techniques, page 9, and prepare your canvas in the same way. Canvas tends to stretch and loose its shape easily. To prevent this, and to make working easier, mount the work on to a large frame.

2 Refer to the Stitch Guide, pages 11–13, for how to work the stitches, and work the design from the centre outwards. Use a large tapestry needle and use a thimble to protect your fingers.

3 Use one strand of tapestry wool (yarn) for the half cross stitch.

4 Stitch the outer border by working 22 rows of half cross stitch using very deep avocado green 7359.

5 To mount the completed embroidery into the firescreen, follow the manufacturer's instructions.

ADDER
The adder is a venomous snake, with hollow fangs that inject venom into its victims, and a distinctive black zig-zag stripe which runs down the length of its back. It eats any small mammals, young birds, slugs, worms and other creeping things. In the cold winter months it hibernates, and emerges in April.

ADDER CUSHION

FINISHED DESIGN SIZE
Without border – 20 x 29cm (7³/₄ x 11¹/₂ in)
approximately

WHAT YOU WILL NEED
◆ Khaki 14-count Aida (Zweigart E3706), 40 x 50cm
  (16 x 20in)
◆ Cotton fabric for backing, 40 x 90cm
  (¹/₂ yd x 36in) wide
◆ Thick furnishing braid, 1.4m (1¹/₂ yd)
◆ Decorative braid or ribbon, 1.4m (1¹/₂ yd)
◆ Polyester wadding (batting)
◆ Matching sewing thread

DMC STRANDED COTTON (FLOSS)
1 SKEIN
Black; white; brown-black 3371; dark caramel 869; med
caramel 420; light caramel 422; pale yellow 745; light
yellow 744; dark saffron yellow 725; light topaz 783; med
topaz 782; dark topaz 781; very dark topaz 780; soft
orange 977; med soft orange 976; chestnut brown 975;
light yellow-green 734; bronze 730; dark ecru 3033; light
brown-beige 3782; med brown-beige 3032; dark brown-
beige 3781; med brown 801; very deep avocado green
934; dark moss green 469; dark brick red 3777; bright
orange-red 606

2 SKEINS
Med yellow-green 733; dark yellow-green 732

1 First, read through Techniques, page 9, and
prepare your fabric. Refer to the Stitch Guide, pages
11–13, for how to work the stitches, and work the
design from the centre outwards.

2 Use two strands of stranded cotton (floss) for the
cross stitch.

3 When you have stitched the design, measure
the width of the decorative braid or ribbon, and
leave a border of Aida fabric, slightly wider than
this measurement. Stitch the outer border by
working two rows of cross stitch in med yellow-green
733, one row in light topaz 783 and finally, two rows
in dark yellow-green 732; then stitch the braid or
ribbon in place by hand or machine.

4 Cut away excess fabric to within 1.5cm (⁵/₈ in) of
the finished design. Cut a piece of backing fabric to
the same size. With right sides facing, pin, tack
(baste) and stitch the cushion front and back
together, leaving a 15cm (6in) gap for turning. Turn
through to right side, fill with wadding (batting),
and slipstitch the opening. Slipstitch the thick furnishing braid round the outer edge.

Opposite: *The Adder Firescreen is worked in tapestry wool
for a luxurious finish.*
Below: *The snake is hidden amongst the leaves of the Adder
Cushion.*

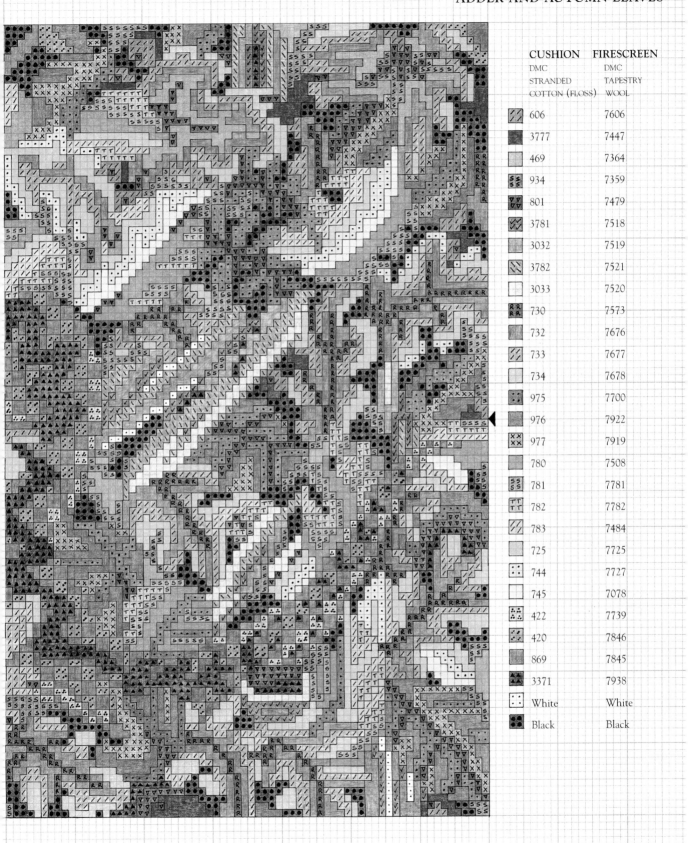

ADDER AND AUTUMN LEAVES

	CUSHION	FIRESCREEN
	DMC STRANDED COTTON (FLOSS)	DMC TAPESTRY WOOL
	606	7606
	3777	7447
	469	7364
	934	7359
	801	7479
	3781	7518
	3032	7519
	3782	7521
	3033	7520
	730	7573
	732	7676
	733	7677
	734	7678
	975	7700
	976	7922
	977	7919
	780	7508
	781	7781
	782	7782
	783	7484
	725	7725
	744	7727
	745	7078
	422	7739
	420	7846
	869	7845
	3371	7938
	White	White
	Black	Black

WINTER

Winter evenings drawing in fast – just the time to indulge yourself in cross stitch. Choose any of our lovely seasonal projects, curl up in front of the fire, and stitch away!

With Christmas and New Year, winter is very much a season of celebration. Use the traditional holly, ivy and mistletoe in 'Winter Leaves and Berries' (page 114) to create your own Christmas cards and decorations. Or make yourself the beautiful waistcoat on page 116, especially for Christmas Day. Pride of place should go to a Christmas cake decorated with a fabulous cake band adorned with sparkly Christmas roses and holly, worked with silk and metallic thread (page 123). The delicate Christmas roses and bright pansies of 'Winter Flowers' (page 107) make pretty trims for a dressing gown and waterbottle cover to keep you warm during the cold winter nights.

With pictures such as the 'Winter Bird Table' (opposite), 'Oscar and Friends' (page 111) and 'Otter on the Seashore' (page 119), this wonderful collection will provide enough inspiration to keep you busy throughout the cold winter months.

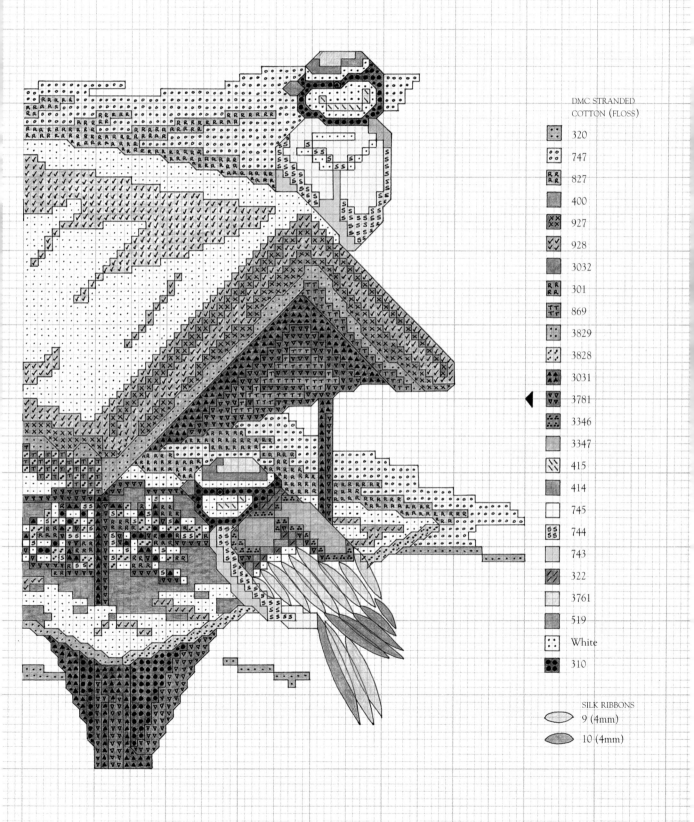

WINTER BIRD TABLE

DMC STRANDED
COTTON (FLOSS)

Symbol	Code
320	320
747	747
827	827
400	400
927	927
928	928
3032	3032
301	301
869	869
3829	3829
3828	3828
3031	3031
3781	3781
3346	3346
3347	3347
415	415
414	414
745	745
744	744
743	743
322	322
3761	3761
519	519
White	White
310	310

SILK RIBBONS

9 (4mm)
10 (4mm)

Winter Bird Table

*This charming snowy scene is the last of the 'Four Seasons' designs, completing the set.
In a typical winter garden scene, the colourful blue-tits flock to the birdtable with its plentiful
supply of nuts and scraps of food, essential to their survival during the cold months.
The birds are worked in cross stitch and three-quarter cross stitch, and silk ribbon embroidery
has been used very cleverly to highlight some of the birds' wing and tail feathers.*

FINISHED DESIGN SIZE
19 x 26.5cm (7^1/$_2$ x 10^1/$_2$ in) approximately

WHAT YOU WILL NEED
- ✦ White 14-count Aida (Zweigart E3706), 38 x 46cm (15 x 18in)
- ✦ 4 tiny black glass beads

DMC STRANDED COTTON (FLOSS)
1 SKEIN
Black 310; white; sky-blue 519; light sky blue 3761; dark azure blue 322; med yellow 743; light yellow 744; pale yellow 745; med steel grey 414; light ash grey 415; light leaf green 3347; med leaf green 3346; dark brown-beige 3781; very dark brown-beige 3031; light toffee 3828; med toffee 3829; dark caramel 869; light mahogany 301; med brown-beige 3032; very light grey-green 928; light grey-green 927; med mahogany 400; light blue 827; very light sky-blue 747; med sage green 320

RIBBON DESIGNS SILK RIBBONS
4mm wide: light blue (colour 9), 1.5m (1^5/$_8$ yd); dark blue (colour 10), 1m (1^1/$_8$ yd)

1 First, read through Techniques, page 9, and prepare your fabric. Refer to the Stitch Guide, pages 11–13, for how to work the stitches and attach beads, and work the design from the centre outwards.

2 Work all the cross stitch areas first, then backstitch detail, and finally fill in the areas of silk ribbon embroidery.

3 Use two strands of stranded cotton (floss) for the main area of cross stitch. Use one strand for the small patches of grass in med sage green 320, the background sky in very light sky-blue 747 and light blue 827.

4 When the cross stitch is complete, add a tiny black glass bead for each bird's eye. Alternatively, work French knots in one strand of black 310.

5 Some of the wing and tail feathers are worked in silk ribbon embroidery to highlight and add texture. The colours and widths of the ribbons used are indicated on the colour key.

6 Refer to Mounting and Framing, page 10, for how to complete your picture.

WINTER BIRD TABLE
In the winter months, many birds and animals are dependant upon the food and scraps that are left out for them. For many small birds, such as blue tits, these scraps mean the difference between life and death.

With a plentiful supply of nuts, suet and water, birds can build up supplies of energy to survive the harsh winter months. Once you start putting food out, it is important to continue to do so throughout the winter, as the birds get used to a regular source of food and rely upon that supply.

Winter Flowers

Flowers, such as pansies, Christmas roses and snowdrops, brighten up the cold, gloomy winter months, bringing with them thoughts of the springtime to come. Here, we've worked dainty winter flowers in simple repeats, creating pretty trims to bring a splash of colour to bedroom accessories. The delicate bookmark is on 40-count silk gauze, so fine that the tiny pansies are worked in half cross stitch.

PANSY WATER BOTTLE COVER

FINISHED DESIGN SIZE
Each flower motif is 1.5cm (⁵/₈ in) square approximately

WHAT YOU WILL NEED
- White 15-count Aida band with white edging (Zweigart E7316), 37 x 8.5cm (14¹/₂ x 3¹/₂ in) wide
- Cotton fabric, 50 x 90cm (⁵/₈ yd x 36in) wide
- Lightweight polyester wadding (batting) 50 x 90cm (⁵/₈ yd x 36in) wide
- Narrow lace edging, 1.6m (1³/₄ yd)
- Narrow ribbon for ties
- Matching sewing thread

DMC STRANDED COTTON (FLOSS)
1 SKEIN
Black 310; white; bright orange 608; dark forest green 987; med tangerine 741; light tangerine 742; med yellow 743

1 First, read through Techniques, page 9, and prepare your fabric. Refer to the Stitch Guide, pages 11–13, for how to work the stitches.
2 Leave 2cm (³/₄ in) at each end of the Aida band, then work the pansy design along the length, repeating the design so that you stitch three rows of pansies.
3 Use two strands of stranded cotton (floss) for the cross stitch and backstitch.
4 Work the trellis in backstitch in dark forest green 987. At the centre of each flower, work a French knot using one strand of black.

TO MAKE THE WATER BOTTLE COVER

1 Use the graph to draw out a template of the water bottle cover pattern (fig 28). Refer to How to Use the Graphs, page 8, for instructions. Cut two pieces each of cotton fabric and wadding (batting).

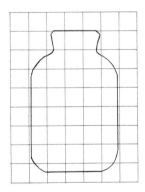

Fig 28: Water bottle template

2 Lay wadding (batting) shapes side by side on a flat surface. With right sides up, place the cotton fabric shapes on top of each wadding (batting) shape. Tack (baste) fabric and wadding (batting) together to form the front and back of the cover. Quilt the two layers by hand or machine.
3 Lay one quilted cotton fabric shape, right side up, on a flat surface. Place the embroidered Aida band right side up, centrally along the length of the fabric. Pin, tack (baste) and machine stitch in place, then stitch lace trim along each long edge of the Aida band.

107

4 Make a 1.5cm (^{5}/$_8$in) hem along the top neck edge and the bottom curved edge of each quilted shape. Then, with right sides facing and wadding (batting) outwards, place the front and back pieces together. Pin, tack (baste) and machine stitch the two pieces together, from the top hemmed edges to the bottom hemmed edges. Trim away excess fabric to 6mm (^{1}/$_4$in) of seam line, then turn cover through to right side.

The simple repeated patterns of winter flowers make a delicate trim for the Christmas Roses Dressing Gown (centre) and Pansy Water Bottle Cover (left), and a single bloom can be worked to decorate the tiny Pansy Bookmark (right).

5 Stitch the lace trim around the top and bottom hemmed edges of the water bottle cover. Add ribbon ties at the bottom edge, insert the water bottle and tie the ribbons to keep the water bottle in place.

CHRISTMAS ROSES DRESSING GOWN

FINISHED DESIGN SIZE
Each flower motif is 1.5cm (⁵/₈in) square approximately

WHAT YOU WILL NEED
- ◆ White 15-count white Aida band with white edging (Zweigart E7107), 5cm (2in) wide to match width of cuffs and pocket and allow for turnings
- ◆ Dressing gown
- ◆ Narrow ribbon and lace for edging
- ◆ Matching sewing thread

DMC STRANDED COTTON (FLOSS)
1 SKEIN
White; dark orange-spice 720; dark saffron yellow 725; very dark forest green 986; med pink-grey 452

1 First, read through Techniques, page 9, and prepare your fabric. Cut the Aida band to the width of the cuffs and pockets, adding a 6mm (¹/₄in) turning at each end. Refer to the Stitch Guide, pages 11–13, for how to work the stitches, and work the designs along the length of the Aida band.
2 Use two strands of stranded cotton (floss) for the cross stitch and backstitch. Work backstitch detail using med pink-grey 452 around the flowers and very dark forest green 986 for the leaf stems.

3 Press from the wrong side, pressing the turnings at each end. Machine or handstitch the band to the cuffs and pockets, then stitch a lace trim along each edge of the band. Finish by stitching narrow ribbon over the seam of the lace.

PANSY BOOKMARK

FINISHED DESIGN SIZE
13mm (⁵/₈in) approximately

WHAT YOU WILL NEED
- ◆ Fine silk gauze, 40-count, to fit size of bookmark
- ◆ Decorative gilt bookmark
  Both available from Elizabeth R Anderson (see Stockists, page 127)

DMC STRANDED COTTON (FLOSS)
Use the list for the pansy water bottle cover

1 First, read through Techniques, page 9, and prepare your fabric. Refer to the Stitch Guide, pages 11–13 for how to work the stitches, and work the deign from the centre outwards.
2 Because the silk gauze is so fine, the design has to be stitched in half cross stitch, using one strand of stranded cotton (floss).
3 To finish the bookmark, mount the embroidery by following the manufacturer's instructions.

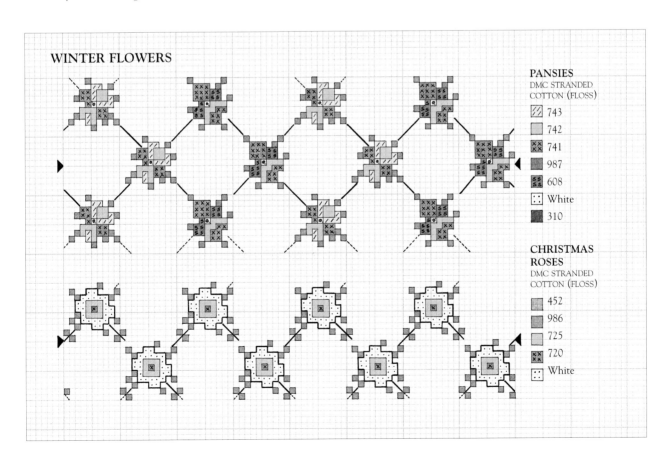

WINTER FLOWERS

PANSIES
DMC STRANDED COTTON (FLOSS)

- ▨ 743
- ▥ 742
- ⊠ 741
- ▩ 987
- ⑤ 608
- ⊡ White
- ■ 310

CHRISTMAS ROSES
DMC STRANDED COTTON (FLOSS)

- ▥ 452
- ▤ 986
- ▢ 725
- ⊠ 720
- ⋮ White

Oscar and Friends

*One of the more ambitious designs in
our book, teddy bear Oscar and his two fluffy
Persian kitten companions will prove to be
firm family favourites.*

FINISHED DESIGN SIZE
25 x 30cm (10 x 12in) approximately

WHAT YOU WILL NEED
◆ White 14-count Aida (Zweigart E3706), 46 x 51cm
(18 x 20in)

DMC STRANDED COTTON (FLOSS)
1 SKEIN
Black 310; white; ecru; brown 433; very dark tan 434;
dark tan 435; medium tan 436; light tan 437; dark cream
738; very dark grey 535; dark cream 938; medium
mahogany 400; light rose 899; medium rose 335; deep
rose 309; very deep rose 326; medium garnet 815; hint of
grey 762; light ash grey 415; light steel grey 318; medium
steel grey 414; dark steel grey 317; charcoal grey 413;
dark gold 782; med topaz 783; light coral 352; peach 353;
brown-black 3371; dark chocolate brown 838; chocolate
brown 839; light mink 842; very light pink-beige 543;
medium leaf green 3346; light leaf green 3347; very light
leaf green 3348

1 First, read through Techniques, page 9, and
prepare your fabric. Refer to the Stitch Guide, pages
11–13, for how to work the stitches, and work the
design from the centre outwards.
2 Use two strands of stranded cotton (floss) for the
cross stitch, and one strand for the backstitch.
3 Work backstitch detail in black 310 to outline the
kittens' eyes and mouth, and Oscar's eyes. Work
long straight stitches, in one strand of white for the
kittens' whiskers and eyebrows, and two strands of
black 310 for Oscar's mouth.
4 Refer to Mounting and Framing, page 10, for how
to complete your picture.

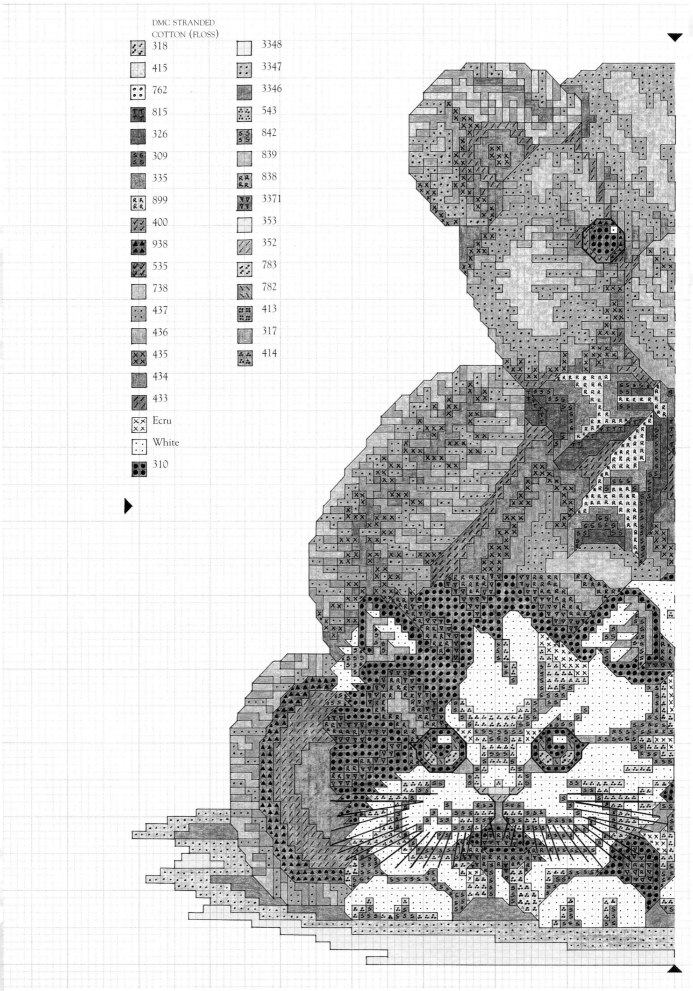

DMC STRANDED
COTTON (FLOSS)

318	3348
415	3347
762	3346
815	543
326	842
309	839
335	838
899	3371
400	353
938	352
535	783
738	782
437	413
436	317
435	414
434	
433	
Ecru	
White	
310	

OSCAR AND FRIENDS

Winter Leaves and Berries

This seasonal collection of winter berries and leaves is perfect for a range of projects: from our stunning waistcoat and hessian Christmas sacks, to Christmas cards.
The lush green leaves, bright red and soft white berries are cleverly mixed with metallic threads to make the whole design really sparkle. These lovely designs are ideal for a variety of Christmas gifts and decorations – let your imagination run away with you!

CHRISTMAS SACKS

FINISHED DESIGN SIZE
6cm (2¹/₄in) approximately

WHAT YOU WILL NEED FOR EACH SACK
- ✦ Scraps of white 14-count Aida for patches
- ✦ Hessian (sacking) fabric, 80 x 115cm (⁷/₈yd x 45in) wide
- ✦ Contrast fabric for cuff, 30 x 90cm (³/₈yd x 36in) wide
- ✦ Lace for trim, 50cm (⁵/₈yd)
- ✦ Gold braid for trim, 50cm (⁵/₈yd)
- ✦ Matching sewing thread

DMC STRANDED COTTON (FLOSS)
1 SKEIN
Mistletoe – white; med leaf green 3346; light leaf green 3347; light yellow-green 734; very light old-gold 677; off white 746; light antique gold 372. **Holly** – white; med pea green 906; very dark pea green 904; very dark forest green 986; bright orange 608; bright orange-red 606; crimson 321; dark brown 898. **Ivy** – very light moss green 472; med moss green 470; dark moss green 469; med avocado green 937; dark avocado green 936

DMC METALLIC THREAD
1 reel (spool): Mistletoe – white 272; multicolour 275; **Holly** – white 272; red 270; green 269; **Ivy** – bright green 278

1 Read Techniques, page 9. Refer to the Stitch Guide, pages 11–13, for how to work the stitches.
2 Make small patches by embroidering a mixture of the small designs on to white Aida, working each design from the centre outwards. Follow steps 3–5 for the winter garland waistcoat (page 118), then trim away excess fabric to leave 7.5cm (3in) squares.
3 The finished size of the sack is 46 x 71cm (18 x 28in). Cut two pieces of hessian (sacking), each 49 x 74cm (19¹/₄ x 29¹/₄in), and one piece of contrast cotton fabric 21 x 49cm (8¹/₄ x 19¹/₄in) for the cuff.
4 To make the sack front, match the wrong side of one hessian shape, with the right side of the cuff fabric, so that one long edge of the cuff matches one short edge of the hessian. Pin, tack (baste) and stitch fabric together along the top edge. Press seam open, then fold the cuff fabric along the seam line to turn the cuff to the right side of the hessian. Press in place, then pin, tack (baste) and stitch the lower cuff edge to the hessian. Stitch the lace and gold braid over this seam line, concealing the raw edges.
5 Pin and tack (baste) the squares randomly on the sack front, then run several rows of machine stitches 6mm (¹/₄in) from the outer edges. Finish each patch by teasing out the threads at the outer edges. The rows of machine stitches will prevent further fraying.
6 Make a 1.5cm (⁵/₈in) hem along one short edge of the remaining hessian shape. With right sides facing, place the front and back pieces together, so that the top edge of the cuff and the hemmed edge match. Pin, tack (baste) and stitch along three edges, leaving the top edge open. Turn sack through to the right side, and stitch a piece of gold braid at one corner to form a hanging loop.

WINTER LEAVES AND BERRIES

MISTLETOE

DMC (FLOSS)	DMC METALLIC THREAD
936	
937	
469	
470	
472	278
898	
321	270
606	
608	
986	269
904	
906	
372	275
746	
677	
734	
3347	
3346	
White	272

HOLLY

IVY

CHRISTMAS CARDS

FINISHED DESIGN SIZE
6cm (2¹/₄ in) approximately

WHAT YOU WILL NEED FOR EACH CARD
◆ White Damask 14-count Aida (Zweigart E3229), 18cm (7in) square
◆ Small scraps of lightweight iron-on interfacing
◆ Cards to mount finished embroidery
◆ Silver token or charm (available from Charland Designs, see Stockists, page 27)

DMC STRANDED COTTON (FLOSS) AND METALLIC THREADS
Use the lists for the Christmas sacks

1 Follow step 2 for the winter garland waistcoat.
2 Use two strands of stranded cotton (floss) for the cross stitch and backstitch. Work backstitch detail in med leaf green 3346 for the mistletoe stems, and med moss green 470 for the ivy stems.
3 Some areas of each design are worked with metallic threads. Use one strand of stranded cotton (floss) combined with one strand of metallic thread. The colour key on the chart lists the shade codes for both.
4 Stitch a small silver charm on to the competed design, then refer to Mounting and Framing, page 10, for how to complete your cards.

WINTER GARLAND WAISTCOAT

FINISHED DESIGN SIZE
9 x 30cm (3¹/₂ x 11³/₄ in) approximately

WHAT YOU WILL NEED
◆ Purchased pattern for waistcoat
◆ Natural 25-count Dublin linen (Zweigart E3604), or other linen or blockweave fabric (refer to pattern for fabric requirements)
◆ Fabric for backing and lining (refer to pattern for fabric requirements)
◆ Buttons (refer to pattern for number of buttons)
◆ Matching sewing thread

DMC STRANDED COTTON (FLOSS)
1 SKEIN
White; med leaf green 3346; light leaf green 3347; light yellow-green 734; very light old gold 677; off white 746; light antique gold 372; med pea green 906; very dark pea green 904; very dark forest green 986; bright orange 608; bright orange-red 606; crimson 321; dark brown 898; very light moss green 472; med moss green 470; dark moss green 469; med avocado green 937; dark avocado green 936

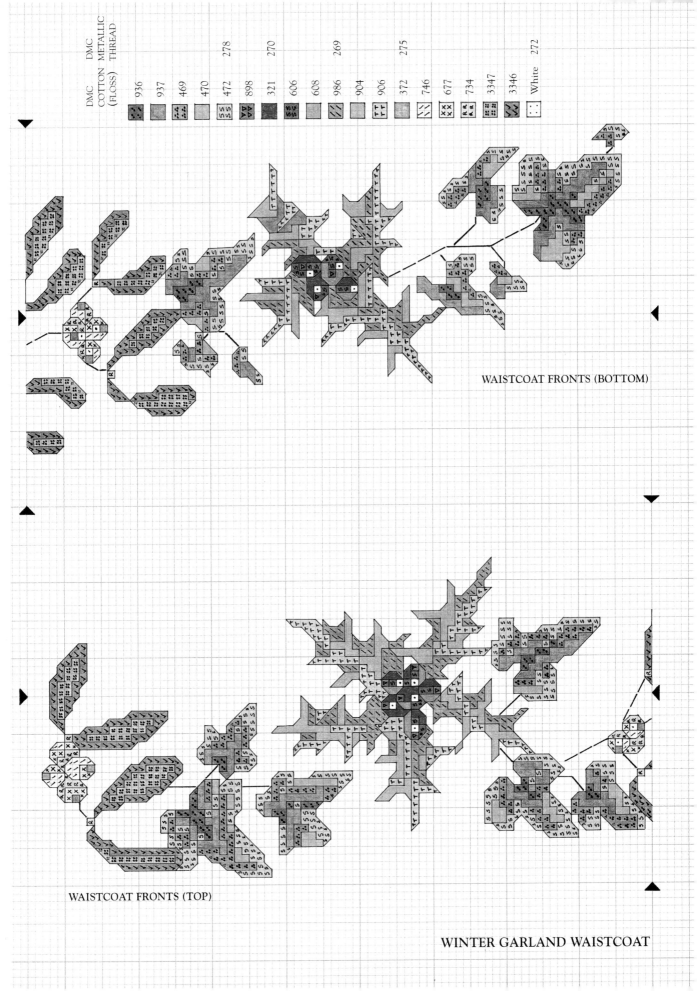

WAISTCOAT FRONTS (BOTTOM)

WAISTCOAT FRONTS (TOP)

WINTER GARLAND WAISTCOAT

The Winter Garland Waistcoat is the perfect garment for Christmas and New Year parties, or just to bring a little sparkle to any winter day.

DMC METALLIC THREAD

1 reel (spool): red 270; green 269; bright green 278; multicolour 275; white 272

1 Lay the pattern pieces for the waistcoat fronts on to the fabric and tack (baste) around their shapes with sewing thread. You may find it easier to stitch the designs on to the fabric before cutting out the waistcoat fronts. If you wish to repeat the design on both sides of the waistcoat, as we have done, the chart needs to be reversed. This can be done by photocopying the chart in reverse.

2 Read through Techniques, page 9. Refer to the Stitch Guide, pages 11–13, for how to work the stitches, and work the design from the centre outwards.

3 Use two strands of stranded cotton (floss), worked over two threads of evenweave, for the cross stitch and backstitch.

4 Some areas of each design are worked with metallic threads. Use one strand of stranded cotton (floss) combined with one strand of metallic thread. The colour key on the chart lists the shade codes for both types of thread.

5 Work backstitch detail in med leaf green 3346 for the mistletoe stems, and med moss green 470 for the ivy stems.

6 Make the waistcoat following the instructions for the purchased paper pattern. Finish by adding buttons which complement the colours of the design, or by adding decorative covered buttons.

Otter on the Sea Shore

Otters are usually found in rivers and estuaries, but during the winter months, when food becomes scarce, they venture down towards the coast in search of fish and crabs. Worked in cross stitch and three-quarter cross stitch, extra sparkle is added by tiny glass beads which have been cleverly used for the frothy tops of the waves.

FINISHED DESIGN SIZE
20.5 x 25.5cm (8 x 10in) approximately

WHAT YOU WILL NEED
+ Grey 14-count Aida (Zweigart E3706), 40 x 46cm (16 x 18in)
+ Chest (from Market Square, see Stockists, page 127)

DMC STRANDED COTTON (FLOSS)
1 SKEIN
White; black 310; ecru; brown-black 3371; dark chocolate brown 838; chocolate brown 839; dark mink 840; med mink 841; light mink 842; very light pink-beige 543; dark donkey brown 3021; dark khaki green 3011; med khaki green 3012; med golden brown 831; very light grey-green 928; light grey-green 927; med grey-green 926; dark grey-green 3768; very dark grey-green 924; dark grey-pink 451; med grey-pink 452; grey-pink 453; light blue-green 504; med blue-green 503; (also, if you work the waves in cross stitch, hint of grey 762 and light ash grey 415)

The foam can either be worked in glass beads or cross stitch. The colour key lists the shade codes for both

MILL HILL BEADS
Glass seed beads – 1 pack: mercury 00283; 2 packs: grey 00150; 3 packs: crystal 00161

1 First, read through Techniques, page 9, and prepare your fabric. Refer to the Stitch Guide, pages 11–13, for how to work the stitches and attach beads, and work the design from the centre outwards. Work the sea foam in either glass beads or cross stitch.

2 Use two strands of stranded cotton (floss) for the cross stitch.

3 To mount the completed embroidery on to the chest refer to the manufacturer's instructions.

OTTERS
Otters, or 'water-dogs', are found in fresh water lakes, rivers, marshes and estuaries. They are powerful swimmers, with webbed feet and fur so dense that water can not penetrate it. Unfortunately the otter population is declining, as they are vulnerable to pollution and disturbance.

OTTER ON THE SEA SHORE

DMC STRANDED
COTTON (FLOSS)

S S / S S	503
R R / R R	504
\ \	453
	452
✓ ✓	451
	924
	3768
	926
	927
	928
	831
	3012
	3011
S S / S S	3021
	543
/ /	842
R R / R R	841
X X / X X	840
T T / T T	839
▼ ▼ / ▼ ▼	838
	3371
o o / o o	Ecru
:.	White
	310

SEA FOAM

	DMC	MILL HILL BEADS
	415	00283
	762	00150
	White	00161

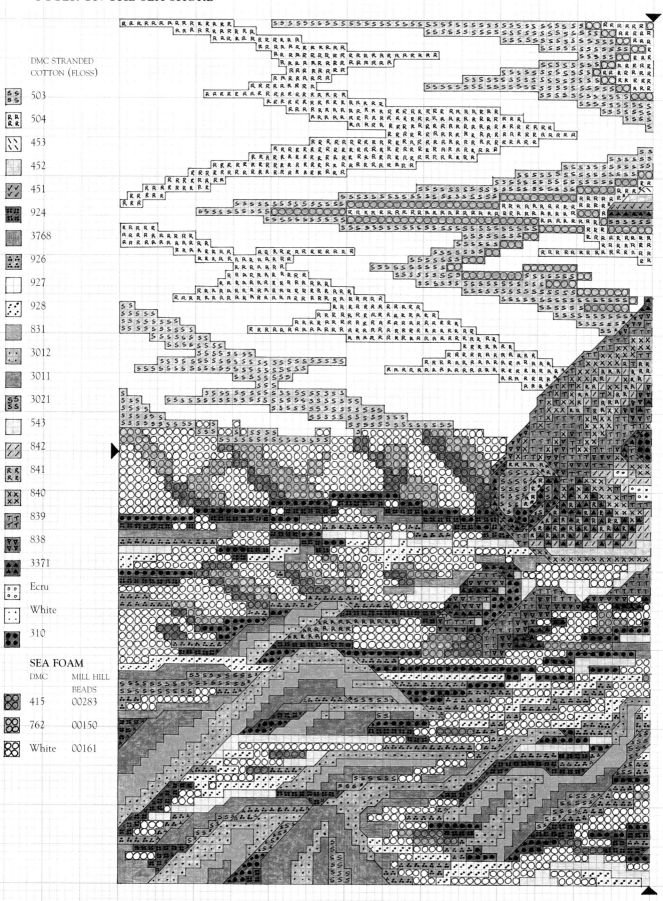

Christmas Roses

Delicate pinky-white petals of Christmas roses, surrounded by rich red berries and vibrant green holly leaves, make a particularly lovely festive cake band. The gold edging of the Aida gives extra Christmas sparkle, making your celebration cake look its very best in the candlelight.

FINISHED DESIGN SIZE
8 x 18cm (3¼ x 7in) approximately

WHAT YOU WILL NEED
◆ White 15-count Aida band with woven gold edging (Zweigart E3716), 8.5cm (3½ in) wide, to fit circumference of cake plus turnings

DMC METALLIC THREAD
1 reel (spool): Metallic gold 284

DMC STRANDED COTTON (FLOSS)
1 SKEIN
White; light topaz 783; very dark orange 946; med pea green 906; bright pea green 907; very light moss green 472; med baby pink 776; light baby pink 818; med pink-beige 950; light pink-beige 3774; dark crimson 304; Christmas red 666; bright orange-red 606; dark jade green 3818; very dark pea green 904; very dark pink-brown 632

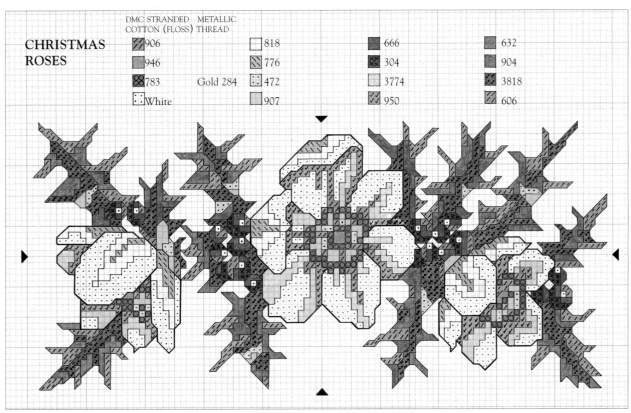

CHRISTMAS ROSES

DMC STRANDED COTTON (FLOSS)	METALLIC THREAD			
906		818	666	632
946		776	304	904
783	Gold 284	472	3774	3818
White		907	950	606

Opposite: *Otter Chest*

1 First, read through Techniques, page 9, and prepare your fabric. Cut the Aida band to the circumference of the cake, adding a 1.5cm (⁵/₈in) turning at each end. Refer to the Stitch Guide, pages 11–13, for how to work the stitches, and work the design from the centre outwards.

2 Use two strands of stranded cotton (floss) for the cross stitch, and one strand for the backstitch.

3 Work backstitch detail around each flower petal in very dark pink-brown 632. Work the stamens at each flower centre in French knots with two strands of metallic gold 284, or two strands of stranded cotton (floss), light topaz 783.

4 Press the band from the wrong side, pressing 6mm (¹/₄ in) turnings at each end. Stitch turnings in place. The cake band is then ready to decorate a Christmas cake.

Christmas Roses Cake Band provides the finishing touch for a perfect Christmas cake.

Templates

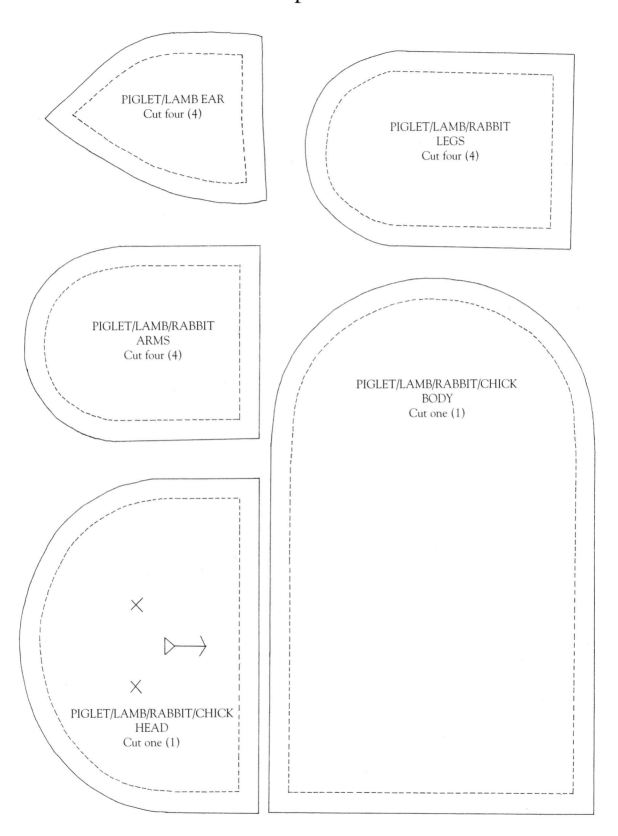

PIGLET/LAMB EAR
Cut four (4)

PIGLET/LAMB/RABBIT
LEGS
Cut four (4)

PIGLET/LAMB/RABBIT
ARMS
Cut four (4)

PIGLET/LAMB/RABBIT/CHICK
BODY
Cut one (1)

PIGLET/LAMB/RABBIT/CHICK
HEAD
Cut one (1)

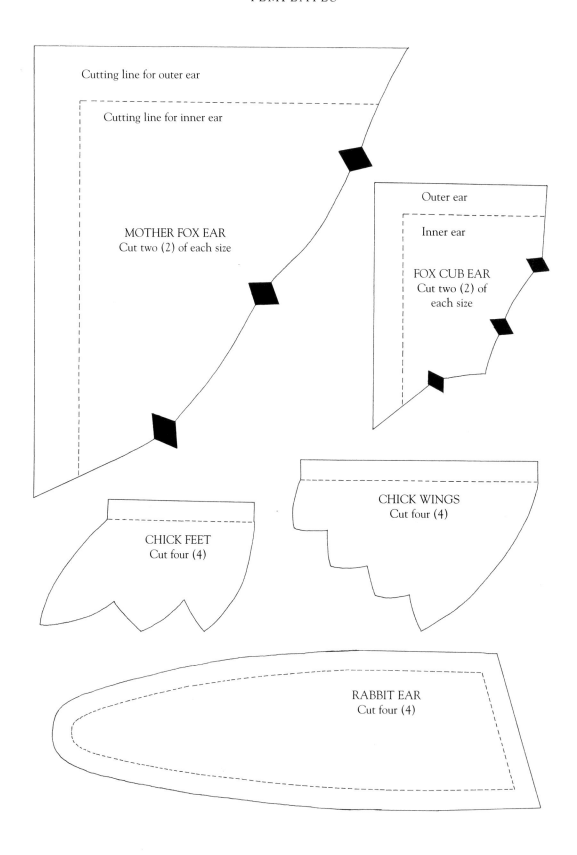

Cutting line for outer ear

Cutting line for inner ear

MOTHER FOX EAR
Cut two (2) of each size

Outer ear

Inner ear

FOX CUB EAR
Cut two (2) of each size

CHICK WINGS
Cut four (4)

CHICK FEET
Cut four (4)

RABBIT EAR
Cut four (4)

Stockists

If you need any further information about products, catalogues, price lists or local stockists from any of the suppliers mentioned, contact them direct by post or phone. Please remember to always include a stamped addressed envelope. If contacting them by phone, they will be able to tell you if there is any charge for the catalogue or price lists.

DMC Creative World, Pullman Road, Wigston, Leicester LE18 2DY, Tel: (0116) 281 1040. For all threads and embroidery fabrics used throughout the book, and the name and address of your nearest DMC and Zweigart stockist.

DMC threads are supplied in the USA by: The DMC Corporation, Port Kearny, Building 10, South Kearny, NJ 07032. Zweigart fabric is supplied in the USA by: Joan Toggitt Ltd, 2 River View Drive, Somerset, NJ 08873.

Framecraft Miniatures Ltd, 372–376 Summer Lane, Hockley, Birmingham B19 3QA. Tel: (0121) 212 0551. Suppliers of the mantle clock, desk accessories, door finger plate, bell pull hanging rods, paperweights and brass pincushion. They also supply **Mill Hill Beads** in the UK.

Framecraft products are also supplied world-wide by: Anne Brinkley Designs Inc, 761 Palmer Avenue, Holmdel, NJ 97733, USA; Gay Bowls Sales Inc, PO Box 1060, Janesville, WI 53547, USA; Ireland Needlecraft Pty Ltd, 4, 2–4 Keppel Drive, Hallam, Vic 3803, Australia.

Laura Ashley Customer Services, Tel: (01686) 622116. Supplied cotton fabrics for the wild flower patchwork quilt and cushions, sunflower collection, 'Down on the Farm', and winter flowers.

Laura Ashley have stores based world-wide, but if you have any enquiries, contact: Laura Ashley Customer Services, 6 St James Avenue, 10th Floor, Boston, MA 02116. Tel: Boston 457 6000; Laura Ashley Customer Services, 24 Luchthavenweg, PO Box 7100, 5500LC Veldhoven, Netherlands. Tel: Veldhoven 563111.

MacGregor Designs, PO Box 129, Burton-on-Trent, DE14 3XH. Tel: (01283) 702117 for mail order catalogue of specialist woodwork accessories. Suppliers of the circular footstool for the summer fruits design.

Market Square (Warminster) Ltd, Wing Farm, Longbridge Deverill, Warminster, Wilts, BA12 7DD. Tel: (01985) 841042. Suppliers of the firescreen for the adder, and the chest for the otter designs.

Elizabeth R Anderson, 'Miniature Embroideries', Rosedale, Tall Elms Close, Bromley, Kent, BR2 0TT. Tel/Fax: (0181) 460 1951. Leading specialists in miniature embroidery, silk gauze, embroidered thimbles, embroidered jewellery, and all fine needlework.

Ribbon Designs, 42 Lake View, Edgeware, Middlesex, HA8 7RU. Tel/Fax: (0181) 958 4966. Suppliers of ribbons for embroidery by mail order, and have the largest range of pure silk ribbons in Europe.

Charland Designs of Canada, suppliers of the beautiful tokens used for the sunflower pincushion, and holly and mistletoe Christmas cards. Available by mail order in the UK from: Silks 'N Sew On, Lion Square, Tywyn, Gwynedd LL36 1DN. Available by mail order in North America from: Charland Designs, 33 Deforest Road, Toronto, Ontario M6S 1 J1 Canada. Tel toll-free: 1 800 567 1789.

Vilene products were used on projects throughout the book. They are available in major department stores and all good haberdashery shops.

Some of the designs included in this book are available in kit form by mail. For further details contact: The Janlynn Corporation, 34 Front Street, PO Box 51848, Indian Orchard, MA 01151–5848, USA. At time of publication, Oscar and Friends was available in kit form.

Acknowledgements

We would both like to give a special thank you to our long suffering husbands, Ian and Tim, for all their support whilst Jayne and I worked frantically on this book. Thank you to our families for being so patient and putting up with us. Thank you also to the following people for their contributions and help with getting this book published: Vivienne Wells, as always; Doreen Montgomery for her invaluable advice and support; Cheryl Brown and Kay Ball at David & Charles for their help and advice with the production of the book. A big thank you to Di Lewis for the wonderful photography, which really makes the book sparkle, and to David Lynch for the photo on the back cover flap. Thank you, also, to Cara Ackerman, Sarah Gray, Elizabeth Anderson, Gleyns Black-Roberts, Susan Haigh, Marilyn Becker and Jacqui Moore. And, finally, a special thank you Sharon Lamb for her stitch work, Stella Nicholas for making the wonderful sugarcraft flowers for the Christmas Roses cake band (page 123), and to John Parkes of Outpost Trading for his excellent picture framing skills, which had to be rushed through at the eleventh hour!

Index